CITIES AND CALIPHS
ON THE GENESIS OF ARAB MUSLIM URBANISM

Nezar AlSayyad

CONTRIBUTIONS TO THE STUDY OF WORLD HISTORY
NUMBER 26

GREENWOOD PRESS
NEW YORK • WESTPORT, CONNECTICUT • LONDON

HT
147.5
.A44
1991

Library of Congress Cataloging-in-Publication Data

AlSayyad, Nezar.
    Cities and caliphs: on the genesis of Arab Muslim urbanism /
Nezar AlSayyad.
        p. cm. — (Contributions to the study of world history, ISSN
0885–9159; no. 26)
    Includes bibliographical references and index.
    ISBN 0–313–27791–5 (alk. paper)
        1. Cities and towns, Islamic—Arab countries—History.
    2. Urbanization—Arab countries—History. I. Title II. Series.
HT147.5.A44 1991
307.76'0917'671—dc20   90–19913

British Library Cataloguing in Publication Data is available.

Library of Congress Catalog Card Number: 90–19913
ISBN: 0–313–27791–5
ISSN: 0885–9159

First published in 1991

Greenwood Press, 88 Post Road West, Westport, CT 06881
An imprint of Greenwood Publishing Group, Inc.

Printed in the United States of America

The paper used in this book complies with the
Permanent Paper Standard issued by the National
Information Standards Organization (Z39.48–1984).

10 9 8 7 6 5 4 3 2 1

3\92

CONTENTS

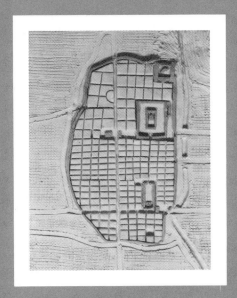

PREFACE

My interest in Islamic cities dates to 1973. As a student of architecture at Cairo University and while studying the history of urban form, I was first exposed to the incredible heritage of the Islamic world. Although my initial reaction was that of fascination, I quickly realized that what I saw around me deserved more than passive appreciation. I continued to be interested in Muslim cities even after I left Egypt in 1979, and three years later I published my first serious work on the streets of Islamic Cairo. As an architect, my concern then was to understand the irregular form of the city and to extract a pattern or a rationale from what appeared to many as capricious disorder. And order there was, for I discovered that the urban fabric of Cairo was not a result of simple accidental accumulation of buildings, but rather a reflection of the Muslim builders' awareness of a variety of physical planning concepts that today we call urban design.

As my readings, travels, and jobs continued to take me to other parts of the Middle East, I became more convinced that Cairo was not an exception, and I decided to expand my research to include other Muslim cities. The current study is an attempt to summarize some of my more recent work. This time, however, my concerns are different. As an urban historian, I am now more interested in the process by which the cities of the Middle East became Islamic. This process, I believe, has not received its fair share of attention in contemporary discourse on urbanism.

One way in which the present work differs from earlier studies of Muslim cities is in its approach to sources. I have attempted to rely almost exclusively on original Arab chronicles. Arab historiography had always fascinated me. Reading the chronicles was not only a search for specific pieces of evidence, but also a spiritual exercise that relaxed my mind. I often allowed myself to get distracted by the wealth of information contained in these chronicles, and it was this flexible approach to them that generated the bulk of this study.

Any work of this kind involves a considerable amount of synthesis. Although I have introduced many new ideas and observations, I have also relied on the work of others and at times repeated positions of a variety of contemporary scholars to create a background for my arguments. My reliance on the chronicles, however, freed me of the unwarranted practice that dictates a comprehensive survey of all the contemporary literature on the many subjects dealt with in this research.

Most of the cities dealt with in this work have changed considerably throughout their history. Since I am only dealing with the process of their initiation, I will be introducing some reconstruction in model and sketch form. I hope that these illustrations in spite of their inaccuracies will help us visualize the form of these cities in their earliest stages.

I have benefited from the help, support, and friendship of a great number of institutions and individuals over the several years it took me to complete this work. I started research on the subject while teaching at the University of Petroleum and Minerals in Dhahran, Saudi Arabia (1982–1985). The library at U.P.M. contained a good collection of the chronicles, and this made it possible for me to read many of them without a preconceived idea or a research agenda. Later, when I moved to the University of California at Berkeley, I was again fortunate enough to find almost everything I needed in the Doe Library. The Graham Foundation for Advanced Studies in the Fine Arts of Chicago provided me with a grant to prepare the illustrations for this book. I am grateful for their support.

I owe a great debt to my mentor, Spiro Kostof, whose advice, encouragement, and friendship has been invaluable in the writing of this manuscript. I wish to express my gratitude to several Berkeley faculty from various departments, including Jean Paul Bourdier from Architecture, Allan Jacobs from City and Regional Planning, Robert Reed from Geography, and Ira Lapidus from History and Middle Eastern Studies. They all provided critical remarks and valuable commentary that gave this work an interdisciplinary dimension. Noeman AlSayyad deserves special acknowledgement. He painstakingly revised and standardized my illustrations and brought the text to life with his rich drawings. My thanks also go to David Moffat and Kaye Bock for editorial assistance. Special credit goes to Annabelle Ison for graphic design assistance, and for helping me produce this manuscript in its final form. At Greenwood Press, Cynthia Harris and Diane Spalding carried the book through its last stages. I am grateful for their input. Finally, I would like to thank my wife, Nadia, for her persistent critique, continuous support, and patient love.

I dedicate this work to my mother and to the memory of my father, whose library collection started me on this path. I hope that my colleagues and students find in this book answers to some of their questions.

NEZAR ALSAYYAD
BERKELEY, JANUARY 1991

CITIES AND CALIPHS

I

PROLOGUE
THE STUDY OF URBAN FORM AND THE PROBLEM
OF THE MUSLIM CITY

The study of Muslim urbanism has been founded on the assumption that Muslim cities are self-contained entities that make up a distinct society and culture radically different from that of other civilizations. Originally introduced by scholars of orientalism in the nineteenth century, the concept of the Muslim city has continued to occupy a central place in urbanist scholarship. It is a concept based on the belief that the Islamic element has had the most profound influence on the historical and physical development of cities in the Middle East.

This book is not a survey of Islamic planning practices. It is a study of the building of the Arab Muslim city and the role played by several caliphs in shaping its urban form. It recognizes the importance of the Islamic component in this process of urban genesis, but it questions the nature of this component. The study suggests that the model of a typical Muslim city consisting of a mosque, a palace, a citadel, and residential quarters is very inadequate. Concentrating on selected Arab Muslim cities, an alternative framework for analyzing and understanding cities of the Islamic Middle East is introduced.

The main agenda set for this research involves a return to the original sources for the study of Muslim cities: the Arab chronicles, particularly those by al-Baladhri (279–892), al-Ya'aqubi (284–897), al-Tabari (310–923), ibn 'Asaker (571–175), and al-Maqrizi (846–1442). Although we may question the authenticity of these writings, they nevertheless remain the most important source for writing about early Muslim urban history. We should remember that the writing of history among the Arabs was a practice that accompanied the cultural development of the Arab Muslim state and although most of these writings were produced by individuals affiliated with one Muslim ruler or another, their authors often attempted to be impartial and balanced. Here again we are reminded that all text is always written with a specific audience in mind and the chronicles are no exception. Many of these chroniclers subjected their sources to some examinations before citing them. The value of an account for the chroniclers depended on the closeness of the source to the original historical incident. When this situation did not exist, they relied on *Isnad*, a system based on a chain of collective consensus.[1] In any case, the inaccuracies in those chronicles do not give us the right to simply dismiss them as unreliable. To attain a degree of consistency in this book, I will try to rely only on stories corroborated by more than one chronicle.

This study will not be based on an exhaustive survey of the contemporary literature nor will it present a comprehensive history of any of the cities included. On reviewing the manuscript for this book, one colleague remarked that this work is more a thesis about history from the point of view of method than it is a professional historical thesis. I intended it this way, because I believe that if we do not reexamine our methods when we write history, then the history we write is of no value except to us, the community of professional historians whose primary concern is the sustenance of our discipline. Throughout the book my central focus will be on the process by which towns were created or appropriated by Islam. The study of Muslim cities is inextricably linked to the lives and actions of those who controlled or governed those cities. Building activity as guided by caliphs, amirs, and other rulers provided the pivotal element of my analysis. By answering the question, "Is there a form for the Muslim city?" I hope to shed some light on another important and relevant question, namely: "What is the Muslim City?"

ISLAM AND URBANIZATION: SOME RELEVANT QUESTIONS

As a religion, Islam started around the beginning of the seventh century A.D. in Arabia. By the end of the eighth century the Islamic empire had extended, reaching India and China in the east and Spain and Morocco in the west. At first, Islamic dominations did not bring about any major physical modifications to the cities and towns, but it introduced a variety of functions to the city. The diversity of conditions in the different Muslim regions led many early researchers to question the existence of Islamic cities with common heritage, characteristics, structure, and form. Indeed, the large Islamic empire was not a monolithic entity. It encompassed different peoples with different original cultures, different economic systems, different national heritages and characters, different climactic and geographical conditions and different strategic defense requirements.

It might then appear that no Islamic city with a universal character, structure, or form could have evolved. While the issue from a scholarly point of view remains unresolved, there is a growing realization that Muslim cities share many characteristics other than the fact that their inhabitants had one common religion. Many scholars have stressed that the differences among those cities should not overshadow the fact that there were more important functional links, shared values, and unifying symbol systems that distinguished those cities from others and allowed them to survive as creative cultural centers.[2]

The expansion of the Muslim Arabs during the seventh and eighth centuries has often been credited with significantly increasing the degree of urbanization in the Middle East and with the introduction of a new urban form, the Muslim city. In a review of recent literature, Wagstaff argues that such a view is unsubstantiable.[3] Protagonists for the traditional position of increased urbanization develop three arguments: the fundamental importance of the city for Islam as a religion,[4] the military needs of the invading Arabs and their settlement policy,[5] and the desires of caliphs and rulers to establish capitals and administrative centers for themselves.[6]

The first argument was challenged by Lapidus, who contended that relatively few towns originated during the Muslim era and that the conquering Arabs did not settle exclusively in new towns.[7] Adams questioned the second argument by pointing out that Islam, especially in Mesopotamia, was not urban and that the establishment of garrison towns simply involved a transfer of population from preexisting surrounding communities.[8] The rationale of the third argument has been questioned by the work of LeTourneau and Hamdan, who argued that all royal towns or government complex towns were either ephemeral creations or twin cities placed alongside already existing ones.[9] Those challenges should not be taken at face value. For example, I believe that a transfer of population from an existing small town to a newly built garrison town, or the establishment of a royal complex that grows rapidly and later blends with the nearby town can still be interpreted as indicators of increased urbanization.

We can reasonably assume that a considerable degree of urbanization accompanied the spread of Islam as a religion and its consolidation as a civilization. For purposes other than those of philosophical argumentation, it does not appear essential for our discussion to establish if Islam was the cause or urbanization was the product. The land of Islam, however, seem to have reached the height of its urbanization trend within three centuries of the introduction of the new religion. In comparing this situation with that of Christian Europe during the Middle Ages, the following points become apparent. First, Christianity as a new religion achieved a similar level of urbanization in a setting that was from the start well urbanized, though not heavily, but this was achieved in almost ten centuries. The second is that urbanization of medieval Europe was more influenced by the revival of Mediterranean trade and the rise of a new political structure of the Middle Ages than it was by the role of the Christian Church.

With regard to Islam's introduction of a new urban form, manifested physically in what is referred to as the Islamic City, Lapidus and Hamdan argued that Islam in most cases simply inherited the forms of the civilization it conquered.[10] Although this is partially true, we should remember that the same applies to the cities of Christian Europe. It was mostly during the Middle Ages that the cultural typology of European cities was established as a function of the layout of open spaces and religious foci.[11] But religion, which played an important role in shaping medieval European city form, was only one among many other factors. It remains important to note that we speak of medieval European cities and not of Christian cities.

But is there a unity in the cities of medieval Europe to allow us to speak of them as a group? At first glance, the answer is not clear! Cities of the Mediterranean shores were different from their counterparts in central and northern Europe. Like the cities of North Africa and the Middle East that were part of the Roman Empire, many of those cities possessed traces of their Roman heritage. Claval tells us that it is the transformation of the urban forms of antiquity that allows us to reply in the affirmative to the question of the identity of the European city. The ancient cities were built around a square, like an agora or a forum. This spatial tradition was continued and preserved by their successors, the Medieval cities of Europe.[12] De Planhol has shown that this tradition died out in such ancient cities when they were conquered by Islam.[13]

Differences in the role played by the religious elements of each city are apparent. For example, unlike the cathedrals and the public palaces of the medieval European city, we may observe that mosques did not always occupy the most favored and visible sites. They did not serve as vistas nor did they acquire on their exterior a nodal public space serving as a collector for all the major roads, as was the case with the medieval European city. Even when they possessed towers that helped a visitor identify their location, these towers or minarets were usually added at later dates.

Here we are confronted with an interesting dichotomy. Muslim society, which accepted strong ties between state and religion, does not appear to have produced a situation similar to that of medieval Europe where the palace and the cathedral played an important visual role representing political and religious power. The absence of an established clerical hierarchy in Islam may explain this difference. The mosque was mainly a social and political institution that did not possess an independent source of authority as did the cathedral. It was primarily the means by which power was transmitted and the place where equality between ruler and ruled was manifested.[14] Why, then, do we refer to cities in the Muslim world as Muslim cities, especially when we know that their religious institutions did not usually serve as centers of institutional power nor did the religious buildings that housed them dominate the urban scene? It is understandable that groups of cities would have their own unique structure because of their existence in a particular geographic region. But the sphere of Islam is vast, and it may not be easily regarded as a single geographic region since it encompasses people of different races and national heritages and lands of different climates and original cultures. Whether Islam was or was not the main shaper of the cities that existed in its sphere is obviously a debatable issue. However, the fact remains that the only solidly observable aspect that allows us to put in one group cities from Morocco to Afghanistan is their existence in the land of earlier Muslim empires from which they may have inherited a specific urban structure unique to Islam and that manifested itself in their physical form. To that structure we may attribute some of the apparent similarities in the form of such cities.

No one has ever put this dichotomy in better words than Janet Abu-Lughod:

> *While the diversity is striking and defies simplification to a single "genre" of either architecture or urban form, it is equally remarkable that one always "knows" when one is in the presence of an Islamic civilization. Is it merely the superficial decoration, the insistently repetitive arches, the geometry of tiny spaces aggregating to vast designs that signal the Code? Is it the basic architectonic concept of square-horizontal and rounded vertical space that announces the unity underlying external diversity in shape? Is it the overall emphasis upon enclosing, enfolding, involuting, protecting and covering that one finds alike in single structures, in quar-*

ters, indeed in entire cities? There appears to be certain basic "deep structures" to the language of Islamic expression in space.[15]

This passionate portrait reflects Abu-Lughod's position regarding the concept of a Muslim city that possesses a unique morphology. A considerable number of scholars who agree with this general conception have advanced descriptions of the Muslim city, its typical elements, physical layout, and spatial structure. In surveying these descriptions we are immediately confronted by the consensus that developed among these scholars regarding the physical form of the city. The typical image goes as follows:

> *The Muslim city is a city whose central node is a Masjid Jami, or Friday mosque, with a well defined and somewhat central royal quarter and a qasabah or a major spine extending from one main gate to another along which lies the most important buildings scattered along the linear bazaar which branches out into the city forming irregular but function-ally well-defined specialized markets. The city also has a citadel or a defensive post on the outskirts and this seems to tie well with its successive walls. Housing was mainly made up of inward oriented core residential quarters, each allocated to a particular group of residents and each is served by a single dead-end street. As for its spatial structure, the Muslim city had no large open public spaces and the spaces serving its movement and traffic network were narrow, irregular and disorganized paths that do not seem to represent any specific spatial conception.*[16]

This description represents the common picture of the traditional Muslim urban settlement, and for the remaining part of this book I will refer to it as the "stereotypical" model. But is this model, commonly used in theorizing, teaching and discussing the Muslim city, an accurate representation of its reality? I think not. And this book goes further to point out that in historical terms, the model is very static and thus inappropriate because it does not take into consideration the factor of time or the nature of urban growth functions. This research will attempt to demonstrate that the stereotypical model is inadequate because it divorces form from function and because as a theoretical construct it is too simplistic to be of any substantial use. By concentrating on the process of urban genesis I hope to introduce a more relevant approach to looking at Muslim cities.

AN APPROACH TO THE STUDY OF URBAN FORM:
ASSUMPTIONS AND RESOLUTIONS

This study is concerned with the form of cities in their cultural context. For this type of research there are a variety of methods to be employed. The most common approach to the history of urban form divides time into established historical periods. Under this approach one may start by analyzing Muslim cities from different regions during a specific historically significant time period. With another common approach one may instead concentrate on the Muslim cities of a given geographic region. In these two approaches a major variable is held constant so that all the others can be observed. Architectural historians are usually more inclined to pursue the former approach, while historical geographers are more interested in the latter.

By combining these two approaches we may get a third approach, one that I call the "thematic" and that I will employ throughout this work. This will be done by examining how specific themes manifest themselves in the develop-ment of the studied cities, regardless of what and where they existed. Because of the nature of the material to be examined, this study attempts to marry different modes of inquiry employed by two separate and usually unconnected disciplines: the practice of urban history and the analytical techniques of urban form and design.

The first task ahead of us here is to find ways of describing and classifying form. "Without a clear analytical system for examining the physical form of a city, it is hardly possible to assess the effect of form. . . ."[17]

According to Lynch and Rodwin, there are a number of criteria that a workable system must first meet before it can be applied: it must apply to cities of different types and scales, it must be capable of being recorded and tested, and it must deal solely with the physical form of the city or with the distribution of activities within it. Although they recognize that cries of dismay may greet such a "narrow" view, they contend that the currently fashionable broader approach to urban form leads to "integrated comprehensive confusion."[18] They then propose a systematic procedure for describing city form and applying it to an imaginary settlement. This model is based on abstract descriptions of various features of the activity pattern and flow system, on the one hand, and of physical form and the distribution of its spaces, on the other.

In his research on the evolution of urban space and the analysis of historic precedents, Roger Trancik identifies three approaches to urban form and design theory: figure-ground theory, linkage theory, and place theory.[19] Although these are different general theories about urban design, taken together they can provide us with potential strategies for integrated urban form analysis. In figure-ground theory, the starting point for an understanding of urban form is the analysis of relationships between solids and voids or building mass and open space. In linkage theory, the key to understanding urban form lies in figuring out the dynamics of circulation and activity patterns. The lines formed by the different city elements to each other establishes the structure of urban form. Place theory goes the further step of adding the components of human functions to a city's cultural and historical contexts. In place theory, social and cultural values, historic significances and visual perceptions of users are the main aspects of our analysis.

In this study I will use a combination of the Lynch-Rodwin analytical system and the linkage and place theories of Trancik's classification. Under this model I will be analyzing a city in terms of solids and voids. Urban solids will be classified into two types: the public institutions that are "object" buildings often serving as centerpieces in the city fabric and acting as visual foci when they are prominently located in space or in a background of solids, and the fabric solids that are the predominant field of urban blocks. The relationship of urban solids to each other will be referred to in this study as the physical layout.

Two types of urban voids will also be considered: the primary circulation network of streets and alleyways, a category corresponding to the predominant field of urban blocks; and the public squares and gardens that are mainly large functional nodes that contrast the large public buildings and provide space for active public life. The relationship of urban voids to each other will be referred to as the spatial structure. The physical layout and the spatial structure make up the city's physical form. Its functional form is made up of the activity and land-use patterns. Urban form encompasses both physical form and functional form (FIGURE I.I)

I will use this analytical model to reconstruct the initial structure of selected cities and to examine the symbolic meaning of their elements. Graphically, this reconstruction cannot, by nature, be exact. And because I will rely on sources of various levels of detail, I will be introducing a graphic notation system to attain some comparative consistency where possible (FIGURE I.2).

To achieve a certain degree of evenness, I decided to choose cities that served relatively similar functions and that had a reasonably large size. Since we are concerned with Islamic appropriation of cities, a process that occurred in different regions at different times, I also decided not to restrict the study to a

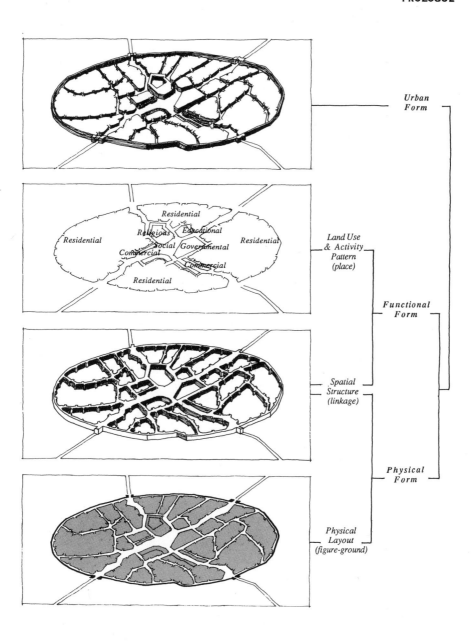

FIGURE 1.1 An Analytical Model for Urban Form Interpretations.

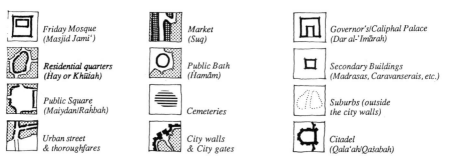

FIGURE I.2 The Graphic Notation System Used for Identifying Muslim City Elements.

specific region or time frame. Cities that served as capitals for their own regions and seats of governments of different Muslim empires provided appropriate case studies for this analytical purpose.

This choice reduced the number of variables involved to a degree that allowed the application of the model while still guaranteeing that certain functions and institutions were always present in each of the chosen cities. Under such a comparison the power structure influencing city form would be adequately represented. Although I have tried as much as possible to abide by these criteria, certain compromises had to be made for lack of information on some cities.

It is impossible to probe many of the issues raised by this work without clarifying definitions, identifying biases, and taking a stand on some of the controversial issues that plague the practice of urban history. These may include questions like: What is meant by the terms *city* and *urban*? How is a city defined? What is the *form of the city*?

While there may be various opinions on these issues, I will in this study use the term *urban* to refer to a condition in which the units of organization within a society become more specialized and more independent and hence more complex. This condition usually occurs as a result of an urban process. *Urbanization* is the spatial manifestation of that process. It is the aggregation of people into relatively large, dense, and heterogeneous settlements. *Urbanism* is often discussed as a result of urbanization, while in fact it is the result of the entire urban process. I will use the term *Urbanism* to refer to the form and culture of the urbanized communities.

Scholars from different disciplines use the term *urban form* or *city form* to mean different things. Most sociologists use it in reference to the structure of urban society. Historians use it when they talk about the urban institutions. I use it here in its most limited sense to mean the physical features manifesting the urban process.[20]

Considerable difficulty attends any attempt to define a city or a town adequately enough to allow a discussion of its morphology over a period of time and in different cultures.[21] In this book a city or a town is defined as a concentration of population larger than its neighboring agricultural hinterland. Its residents are a substantial nonagricultural population concerned with administration, religion, commerce, industry, and defense. And as an entity it possesses physical features that distinguish it from its surrounding countryside.[22]

Our last problem concerns the usage of the term *Muslim* city. As discussed earlier, it may be that the Muslims, even today, continue to be organized in ways more directly linked to religious values and institutions than Christians, Hindus, Buddhists, or any other group with a strong religious base.[23] Nevertheless, to label everything "Muslim" or "Islamic" assumes a poverty of cultural response that does an injustice to the Muslim people and their rich cultural heritage.[24] In this study, the term *Arab Muslim* is used for convenience only. It simply designates cities that were built or taken over by the early Muslim Arabs in the central Middle East. The term *Muslim Arabs* refers to the armies and tribes of Arab origin that adopted Islam and used it as a platform for their conquest of the Central Middle East.

We should remember that no exploration in urban form is free of bias or intent and this book is no exception. Throughout the work I have assumed that the institutional structure of a given society influences the shape of its urban form. Urban form, in turn, is considered to be representative of the larger sociocultural mechanisms that sustain urban existence. I realize the relativity of this assumption and the fact that it may manifest itself in varying degrees in different cultures. However, I decided not to let this obstacle hinder my inquiry.

The book starts by presenting a historiography of the concept of the Muslim city, demonstrating how the development of the concept was paralleled by the development of descriptions of its physical form. In the first part, the stereotypical model of a Muslim city with a central mosque, citadel, palace, segregated residential quarters, and a centralized bazaar is examined and is found to be a very static and inadequate description of its physical reality. Three distinctive types of Arab cities—the garrison town, the transformed town with pre-Islamic origin, and the new capital—are then recognized and each type is examined in turn.

When garrison towns, military camps established by the Arabs during the early conquests, were examined, the investigation revealed that their building methods and their physical forms were products of a process of negotiations between the caliph, the regional governor, and the actual inhabitants.

Scanning the transformation that took place in existing towns taken over by the Muslim Arabs revealed some consistent developmental patterns. These patterns appear to have been part of an unselfconscious program conceived by the caliphs to bring about the Islamization of the city fabric. The resulting development does not seem to represent any Islamic planning ideology but was rather reflective of the changing challenges faced by Arab caliphs attempting to consolidate their reigns.

The analysis of new capital towns, built exclusively as seats of caliphal governments, revealed that their initial forms were mainly a product of elaborate acts of single individuals. Those forms were not representative of any Arabic or Islamic ideals but were physical expressions of symbolic power and politico-religious authority.

The book concludes by suggesting that the Arabs', particularly the Caliphs', changing perception of the role of buildings and their recognition that architecture is of major political value were major factors behind the changing urban forms of Arab Muslim cities.

II

THE TYPICAL MUSLIM CITY
A HISTORIOGRAPHY OF A CONCEPT

*No scholar or school is a perfect representative of some ideal
in which by virtue of national origin. . . he participates.*[1]

EDWARD SAID

The concept of the Islamic city has been with us for almost seven decades
and has recently been receiving its fair share of attention from scholars
from many disciplines. The development of the concept paralleled the
development of descriptions of the physical qualities of the typical Muslim city.

As we discussed earlier, the typical Muslim city was identified as an inward-
oriented city with a Friday mosque and a market bazaar at its center. Its
circulation network was made of narrow irregular streets leading to segregated
residential quarters, and somewhere on the outskirts there was a citadel. This
became the stereotype! Who introduced it? When and why? Was this stereotype a representation of the historical reality of some Muslim cities as they were
observed by ancient travelers, for example, or was it a standardized mental
picture held in common by members of a particular group or discipline and
representing an oversimplified and uncritical judgment?

It is difficult to discuss the origins of the stereotype without a discussion
of the evolution and development of the general concept of the Muslim City
with all the unique circumstances and special traditions that generated it. As
Abu-Lughod reminds us:

> *In some ways, historiography takes the same form as the traditions of
> the Prophet. The authenticity of any proposition is judged by the
> "chain" or isnad by which it descended from the past. Certain chains are
> deemed more trustworthy than others. One makes reference to an earlier
> authority in order to substantiate a statement's authenticity or truth.
> The truth, therefore, is only as good as the chain of its construction.*[2]

Although this was primarily a remark about the original Arab chronicles, Abu-Lughod has shown that this situation also applies to Western scholarship concerned with the construction of the Muslim reality. In this chapter I will primarily build on Abu-Lughod's work by concentrating on both Eastern and Western research relating to the physical form of the Muslim city.

EARLY IDEAS: THE INTRODUCTION OF THE STEREOTYPE

The first interest in the concept of the Muslim city dates back to the early decades of this century and is represented in the works of the Marcais brothers, Sauvaget, LeTourneau, and Von Grunebaum. Of course, this first generation of researchers provided us with basic notions without which further work would have been difficult. And although much of the writing of this early group was produced from a colonialist perspective, it is useful to examine the specific research themes and methodologies used in relation to the types of questions asked then. In fact, the answers that were offered in response to some of these questions had a strong influence on our current understanding of Muslim cities. For example, let us look at the work of the Marcais brothers. Being among the earliest in the field, they are always cited in the introductions to books and articles on Muslim cities.

In a 1928 article, William Marcais introduced for the first time several concepts that were adapted by many scholars at later times.[3] In this article, he pointed out that Islam is essentially an "urban" religion that produced a civilization whose essence was its cities. He reminded us that Muhamad, the prophet of Islam, and his early caliphs were all members of the urban bourgeoisie of Arabia. He also observed that the Friday prayer in the congregational mosque was a reflection of the necessity for urban congregation and for the continued survival of the Islamic religion. In his attempt to identify the physical elements of typical Muslim city, William Marcais describes the quintessential Islamic city which is made of a *Masjid jami* or Friday mosque with a nearby *suq* or market and surrounded by a series of *hamams* or public baths. Although this description was very elementary, it became the nucleus upon which other scholars made further additions to generate the stereotype.

The ideas introduced by William Marcais in the 1920s were followed up by those of his brother George in the 1940s. In two articles written in 1940 and 1957, George Marcais discussed some of the same issues alluded to earlier. On Islam's relationship to cities, George Marcais, like his brother, adopted the position that Islam is essentially an "urban" religion and that the mosque, as a function, "created" the Muslim city.[4] To comply with the earlier attempts to construct the Muslim city, George noted the importance of the market and the baths, but he added three other physical qualities: the differentiation between commercial and residential quarters; the segregation of residential quarters according to ethnicity or specialization; and a hierarchical order of trades in the market, maintaining the cleaner trades closer to the mosque. This important description by George Marcais reads as follows:

> *In the heart of the city there is the Friday mosque which is the religious, intellectual and political center of Muslim life. Near the mosque, as a religious center, we find the* suq *of sacred items where merchants sell candles, incenses, and perfumes. Also near the mosque, as an intellectual center, we find the book sellers and the book binders. As we go further from the mosque, we find the* suqs *of cloth and leather which were often located in secure places encircled by walls called* qaisariya. *Beyond the textile trades we find the markets of the jewelers, the furniture makers and the kitchen utensils. Near the gates, we find the weekly market where goods from the countryside are sold. Finally, on the periphery, we find the industrial trades like the blacksmiths, the dyers, and the tanners.*[5]

From this statement we can see that after adopting the description of the typical Muslim city advanced by his brother William a decade earlier, George's main contribution was the elaborate description of the typical Muslim market. Here it is important to note that all of the examples used by the Marcais brothers, as Abu-Lughod remarked, are unique to the Maghreb and not generally used in other regions.[6] She goes on to conclude that in spite of that, this physical form of the typical Muslim city set forth by the Marcais brothers was adopted by most scholars in the course of time. This was the first step in the construction of a mental image or stereotyped Muslim city and the development of a set of physical and visual myths relating to its urban structure (FIGURE 2.1).

Before we proceed to trace the development of the stereotype, it may be necessary for us first to examine some of the paradigms upon which their work was based. For example, in adopting the view that the city is necessary for an Islamic way of life, George Marcais was, in fact, using an earlier link in the chain of orientalist scholarship, as is evident in his choice of quotations. An example of that is what he says about the Mosque, where he quotes the following from Ernest Renan: "The mosque, like the synagogue and the church, is a thing essentially urban. Islamism is a religion of cities."[7]

This quotation, taken from the work of a renowned Western philologist, is very revealing because it makes us aware of the fact that attempts to define the unique character of the Muslim city were actually rooted in Western philosophical scholarship. With this as a starting point we should not be surprised to find out that the whole enterprise of understanding the Muslim city was based on its juxtaposition with its medieval European counterpart. In other words, the concept of the Muslim city was invented by scholars who were only capable

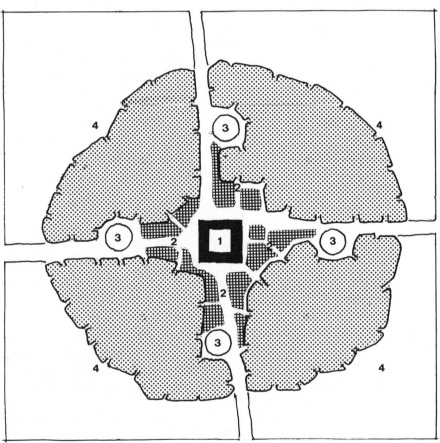

1. Friday Mosque (Masjid Jami') 2. Market (Suq) 3. Public Bath (Hamam) 4. Residential quarters (Hay or Khutah)

FIGURE 2.1 The Stereotypical Muslim City of North Africa Based on Text by W. Marcais (1928), G. Marcais (1945), R. LeTourneau (1957), and J. Berque (1958). (Author's sketch)

of describing this urban entity using norms and standards developed elsewhere. Those scholars were, in fact, unequipped with some of the current methodological approaches that may have allowed them, had they been available, the chance to define such an entity in terms of itself. Of course, there is nothing wrong with observing the Muslim city in a comparative context as those early scholars were attempting to do. The problem existed because such observations were not incorporated in any appropriate comparative framework and were mainly a reflection of Western modes of representation.

Also, in the work of the Marcais brothers, it is important to note that little or no reference is made to the institutional structure or social organization of the Muslim city. This again should draw our attention to another fact, namely, that the origins of the stereotype are rooted in formalist tradition. The Marcais brothers seem to have mainly been interested in interpreting the Muslim city through an identification of its physical components. They used the city to understand urban form and not vice versa. They chose not to confront the issue of what constitutes the essence of Islamic urban existence and instead concentrated their attention on documenting the physical manifestations of that existence.

The work of Roger LeTourneau and Jacques Berque represents a continuation of the tradition set forth by the Marcais brothers. LeTourneau's work on Fez, later culminating in his book on the Muslim cities of North Africa, constituted another attempt to identify a general morphology for the Muslim city based on the concept of cumulative research. Under LeTourneau, the stereotype remained unchanged but is slightly modified so as to accommodate Fez of the Middle Ages. In fact, the physical characteristics of Fez are generalized and applied to all cities of North Africa.[8] This was also the situation of Jacques Berque whose work again borrowed a lot from the Marcais brothers. In attempting to answer the question of what makes the Muslim city in the Maghreb, Berque cited the three typical elements — the Friday mosque, the market, and the public bath — in exactly the same order as that of William Marcais. Berque, however, added a discussion on the functions of the city, because to him the Muslim city served as a place for witness and an arena for exchange, and the above three elements served mainly these two functions.[9]

From all of these examples from North Africa as investigated by the Marcais, LeTourneau and Berque, we are presented with the first phase of the stereotype. This, however, was not to stay with us for long, because in the heart of the Middle East the story was taking a different turn.

ORIENTALIST SCHOLARSHIP: THE DEVELOPMENT OF THE STEREOTYPE

I have discussed, until now, the evolution of a stereotype based on examples from the Maghreb, where most cities grew as a result of a spontaneous accretive process. In the heart of the Middle East most important cities had strong roots in pre-Islamic urban traditions. But the Maghrebi stereotype could not be easily applied to the cities of Syria or Palestine. This was certainly on the mind of Jean Sauvaget when he started his work on Damascus and Aleppo, two cities with a highly ordered geometric plan from Greco-Roman times. Sauvaget discovered that the Greco-Roman geometric block structure had started to decompose with the decline of the Byzantine Empire. He insisted, however, that the radical alteration of the plan was consummated under the Arab-Muslim rule.[10]

In seeking to find out how the process of change in the city took place, Sauvaget identified the first element of his typical Muslim city, the Muslim *suq*, which developed out of the colonnaded avenue of the Byzantine town. Sauvaget also identified other elements in Muslim Aleppo and Damascus: the mosque, which occupied the place of the former church or temple; the central square from pre-Islamic times, which disintegrated into a network of alleyways serving a variety of commercial and residential functions; and the citadel, which usually occupied the hilly site of the ancient defensive post. Although Sauvaget did not produce a diagram of typical Muslim city, his conclusion could be summarized in diagrammatic form (**FIGURE 2.2**).

It is interesting to note in this diagram that the *suq* takes a linear form, the mosque is not necessarily located at a central place, and the citadel is located in the east. This structure provided the basis for the stereotype in the Middle East and was one of the pillars upon which the renowned orientalist Gustave Von Grunebaum based many of his writings about the structure of the Muslim city.

Von Grunebaum, who came to the United States from Germany, fleeing World War II,[11] produced a solid set of articles within the orientalist tradition that dealt with Islam as holistic culture. Perhaps his classic article, "The Structure of a Muslim Town," had more influence on scholars studying the Muslim city than any other piece of work by any of his contemporaries.[12]

This article, commonly used in teaching the Muslim city to students of Muslim civilization, is worthy of some critical analysis. Von Grunebaum starts the article with the story of the Arab geographer Yaqut (1229), who took to task the great literary scholar al-Hariri (1122) because of the latter's classification of a certain place in Iraq as a town.[13] Von Grunebaum continues the story by informing us that Yaqut's objections centered around the fact that this place lacked the two indispensable qualities of townships — a Friday mosque and a permanent market. He then proceeds to describe the typical Muslim town. The following quotations virtually identify his conceptions:

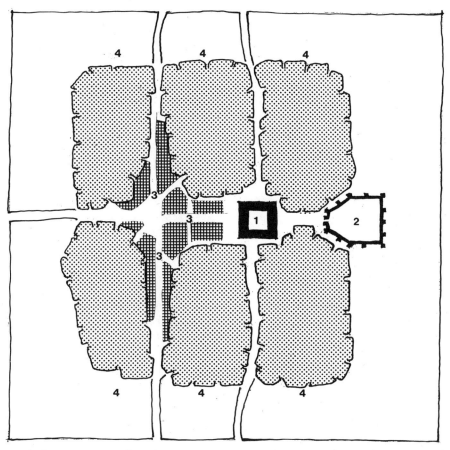

1. *Friday Mosque (Transformed Church)* 2. *Citadel/Palace (Old Defense Post)* 3. *Market (Transformed Colonnade)* 4. *Residential quarters*

FIGURE 2.2 The Stereotypical Muslim City of the Middle East, Based on Sauvaget's Text (1934–1941). (Author's sketch)

The full fledged Muslim town has two focal points: the Friday mosque and the market. The Jami, *as the spiritual center, is appropriately placed along the main thoroughfare or when the plan of the town permits, at the rectangular crossing of the two main thoroughfares which is marked by a spread-out Senate.... Next to the* jami, *we find the principal government building, be it the palace of the ruler or the official residence of his deputy. The* jami *is the political as well as religious center of the settlement. There it is where the inhabitants will gather to hear the proclamations of their rulers and while they will not debate or vote, they will on occasion demon-strate their political will.... It is in the cathedral mosque that the* Katib *or preacher calls down the Lord's blessing on the ruler.... The mosque is also the intellectual center of the town. The* ulama *will assemble in it to discuss and teach.*

Near the mosque as a religious center we will find the suppliers of the sanctuary, the suq *of the candle merchants, the dealers in incense and other perfumes. Near the mosque as an intellectual center we will find also the* suq *of the booksellers, the* suq *of the bookbinders, and as its neighbor, the* suq *of the leather merchants.... Adjoining the group of markets, we enter the hall of the dealers in textiles, the* qaisariyya, *the only section of the* suqs *which is regularly roofed.*

Approaching to the gate of the town one will find, apart from the Caravanserais for the people from the rural districts, the makers of saddles and those of pack-saddles.... Then the vendors of victuals brought in from the country who sometimes will form a market outside the gates.... together with the basket makers, the sellers of spun wool and the like.

On the periphery of the town will be situated such industries as require space and whose vicinity might be considered undesirable; the dyers, the tanners and almost outside the city limits, the Potters.[14]

After careful examination of this entire passage, we first notice that Von Grunebaum used several familiar statements without any reference to their origin. Only at the end of the passage does he provide a reference note, identifying a few relevant books. Second, we realize that Von Grunebaum simply incorporated these quotations into his text without any critical comment, and in doing so contradicted himself because he first identified the mosque and the market as the two "focal points" of the city, but then later suggested that the mosque is placed along the main thoroughfare which is already the market. Third, we detect a considerable similarity between Von Grunebaum's description of the typical Muslim town and the earlier descriptions provided by the Marcais brothers regarding the towns of the Maghreb. Not to our surprise we find in Von Grunebaum's reference notes mention of an article by George Marcais and another by Jean Sauvaget, to whom we attributed the quotations.

Finally, we also discover some major items in Von Grunebaum's description that were not mentioned by either Marcais or Sauvaget, namely that "the Friday mosque is placed along the main thoroughfare or at the rectangular crossing of the two main thoroughfares which is usually marked by a spread-out square," and that "near the *jami* we find the principal government building or palace of ruler." In general, we also notice that Von Grunebaum gives little or no examples of the cities he is describing.

In the rest of the article, Von Grunebaum discussed the workings of the Muslim town, whose unity to him was functional, not civic. He made the point that the Muslim city did not represent a uniform type of civilized life as did the Greek or Roman town.[15] He ended the article by suggesting that ethnic, tribal, and occupational segregation in the residential quarters, the lack of established municipal organization, and a guild-like socioeconomic structure were the main forces behind the shape of the Muslim town.

The picture painted by Von Grunebaum of the typical Muslim town is one that was arrived at by accumulation. First, he accepted the elements of the Muslim city identified earlier by French scholars working on the *Maghreb* — the mosque, the market, and the baths. Then he modified the structure of those elements and their relationship to each other, using the work of another French scholar working on Syrian cities, as with the case of the converted mosque, the linear bazaar, and the citadel. Finally, he added some elements and relationships of his own, for example: the two major thoroughfares intersecting at a central square, the Friday mosque located along the main thoroughfare, and the governor or deputy's palace located next to the *jami* (FIGURE 2.3).

This description of the physical form of the Muslim city by Von Grunebaum is mainly a reflection of the conciliatory nature of his scholarship. His desire to be an impartial scholar-observer led him to the practice of jamming together all research material available at the time without any critical evaluation. Von Grunebaum had no difficulty presuming Islam to be a unitary phenomenon incapable of development, about which he continued, from the beginning to the end of his career, to make a set of reductive negative generalizations.[16] His work on the structure of the Muslim city is no exception to that pattern.

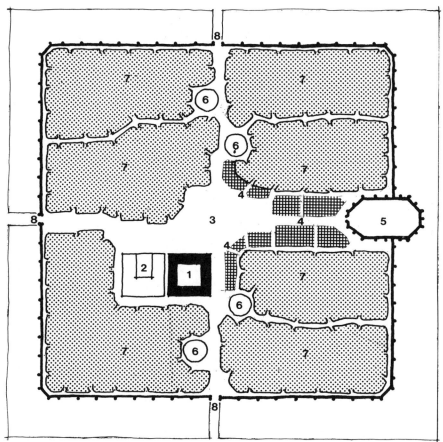

1. *Friday Mosque (Masjid Jami')* 2. *Palace (Dar al-Imarah)* 3. *Public Square (Maiydan)*
4. *Market (Suq)* 5. *Citadel (Qala'ah Qasabah)* 6. *Public Bath (Hamam)* 7. *Residential
quarters* 8. *Walls & Gates*

FIGURE 2.3   The Stereotypical Muslim City of the Middle East, Based on Von Grunebaum's
Text (1955). (Author's reconstruction)

THE CONSOLIDATION OF THE STEREOTYPE AND THE MULTINATIONAL LITERATURE

Because of its plain nature and due to the simplicity of its terms, the
stereotype developed by Von Grunebaum was adopted by many scholars of
Muslim urbanism from both East and West. This could be observed in the work

of Arab and Oriental scholars such as Jairazbhoy, Ismail, and Monier, whose research was a product of the mid– and late 1960s. This same era also witnessed writings by many orientalists, most of whom were still drawing upon one another in a chain of authority that takes them all back to Von Grunebaum.

Searching for what he calls "the traditional Muslim city," Xavier De Planhol, a famed orientalist, contrasted new towns established by the Muslim Arabs with older Greco-Roman towns taken over by them. Except for a detailed discussion of the spatial structure of Muslim cities, De Planhol seems to have fully adopted the Von Grunebaumian stereotype. Assuming that the regularity and uniformity of the ancient European city is the norm, De Planhol makes a serious charge regarding the general organization of the Muslim town:

> *Irregularity and anarchy seem to be the most striking qualities of Islamic cities. The effect of Islam is essentially negative. It substitutes for a solid unified collectivity, a shifting and inorganic assemblage of districts; it walls off and divides up the face of the city. By a truly remarkable paradox this religion that inculcates an ideal of city life leads directly to a negation of urban order.*[17]

A few years later, these accusations were addressed by a scholar from the Orient. In his book *Art and Cities of Islam*, Jairazbhoy, using examples from Mughal India and the Arab Middle East, argues:

> *First of all irregularity has always been alien to Islamic art, and indeed in architectural designs there is usually an over-zealous desire for symmetry. The irregularities of streets in Muslim towns are the result of subsequent haphazard growth and the absence of controlling authority. It is people who are at fault, not the system, which is itself clear, consistent and rational. Because of its very desire for clarity and logic, and because it respects the different ways of living of different races and religion, Islam was anxious to ensure the independence and safety of the inhabitants; racial segregation was a recognition of the innate desire of peoples to live amid their own kind; and the grouping of crafts resulted in competition fair pricing, and ease in locating any object the buyer might require. These are the real reasons the Islamic town took the character that it did.*[18]

Of course, all of this is very good, but if we review the typical elements of the Muslim city and its overall organization as identified by Jairazbhoy, we will notice a striking similarity to the Von Grunebaumian stereotype:

> *It is natural to speak first of the fortified walls. . . . Cities usually had a
> citadel serving as the focus of defense and containing the governor's resi-
> dence. . . . The quarters of the Islamic Cities were assigned on a tribal,
> ethnic or religious basis. . . . Another typical characteristic of Islamic
> cities is the hierarchic arrangements of trades, starting from the Great
> Mosque . . . . The Friday mosque was often located in the market
> place. . . . at the center of the town. . . . In the larger towns, the
> government house was built close to the chief mosque.[19]*

A further check of Jairazbhoy's references reveals that although he did not
rely on Von Grunebaum (he only cites him once), he used exactly his same
sources. In fact, Jairazbhoy's major statements about the elements of the typical
Muslim city could be easily traced back to Marcais, Sauvaget, and Massignon,
whom as I have shown earlier were Von Gruenbaum's original sources.

In fairness, however, it ought to be mentioned that Jairazbhoy provides us
with more accurate information, mainly from early Arab travelers' accounts,
which may substantiate Von Grunebaum's contentions. Jairazbhoy's contribution would have been more substantial had he ignored Von Grunebaum's work
altogether and started from scratch using those original travel accounts. The
hidden influence of the Von Grunebaum tradition in Jairazbhoy's work makes
it another addition to the chain of scholarly orientalist authorities reconstruct-
ing the reality of the Muslim city.

At the time when Jairazbhoy's book, published in India, was spreading the
Von Grunebaumian stereotype in that part of the world, the work of Monier and
Ismail was carrying on the same task in the Middle East. Monier, an Arab
architectural historian working in Lebanon, followed suit in describing a typical
Muslim city that is based on the Von Grunebaum type.[20] In fact, if we compare
his diagrammatic plan of a typical Muslim city to the Von Grunebaumian
stereotype, we find a great deal of similarities (FIGURE 2.4). For example, the
city has two major thoroughfares with the bazaar extending along one of them.
At the intersection are the most important public buildings and the Friday
mosque. The citadel is on a neighboring hilly site adjacent to the city. Again,
all of those elements are present in the Von Grunebaumian stereotype, though
the order is slightly different. Monier seems to have been more influenced by the
case of Cairo, to which he devotes a considerable attention, and his diagrammatic plan of a typical Muslim city seems to replicate the exact elements, order,
and topography of medieval Cairo.

Ismail's work on the origin, ideology, and physical patterns of Arab
urbanization represents another addition to the constructivist chain.[21] This work,

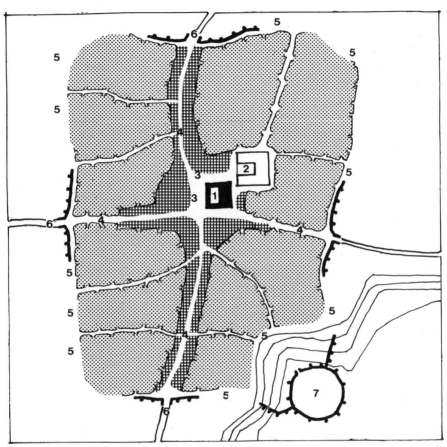

1. Main Mosque 2. Royal Quarter 3. Market/Suq 4. Main Thoroughfare 5. Residential quarters 6. Walls & Gates 7. Citadel

FIGURE 2.4 A Diagramatic Plan of a Typical Muslim City, According to Monier (1971). (Compare to the diagrams of medieval Cairo in CHAPTER 5.)

originally a doctoral dissertation at the University of Karlsruhe in Germany, follows the same path as all the others except that Ismail was more interested in looking at the broader picture and at a longer time-frame.

Based on the work of early Arab geographers, Ismail presented us with a discussion of settlement types, ranks, and sizes. This framework, he believed, must qualify any serious study of the form of the Arab city. Looking at three cities as case studies, he proceeded to discuss the different institutions of the

Arab-Muslim city and its physical elements. Again, he identified an inner core containing a central mosque with a square or *maiydan* adjacent to it and a market or *suq* branching out of it with *hamams*, or baths, and *Qaysariyas*, or *caravansari*, close by. This was surrounded by residential quarters, engulfed by a wall, open markets, industries outside the gates, and finally a citadel containing the major governmental buildings (FIGURE 2.5). Ismail then introduced nicely drawn schematic plans of the Medieval Arab city showing several stages of its urban growth. It is obvious that Ismail's diagram is merely a well-articulated visual representation of the Von Grunebaumian stereotype.

Perhaps no single scholar has contributed more to the consolidation of the stereotype than Albert Hourani, who organized in the late 1960s one of the first scholarly symposia on Islamic urbanism. A few years later, the symposium papers were published in the often-cited *The Islamic City*.[22] In the introductory article, Hourani confronted the issue of what makes the Muslim city. To resolve this problem he referred to Max Weber's critical components or marks of a city. He made the point that although Islamic cities may have lacked some of Weber's marks, they were still able to flourish and maintain a high level of urban activities. After warning us about the innumerable variations in city form, Hourani constructed a picture of what a typical Islamic city looked like. In his words:

> . . .*speaking very roughly, we may say that we should expect to find such features as the following. First, there would be a citadel, very often placed on some natural defense work, and serving indeed to explain why there is a city at all in that place. . . . Secondly, there might be a royal "city" or "quarter" which would have grown up in either of two ways. . . . It might be a royal enclave implanted in an already existing urban conglomeration, or it might be a new foundation on urban soil and around which a conglomeration later grew, attracted by the power, wealth and prestige of a court. However it began, it tended to be more than a palace: it would be rather a "compound," grouping royal residence, administrative offices, places for the bodyguard or personal troops. . . . Thirdly, there would be a central urban complex, which would include the great mosques and religious schools, and the central markets with their khans and qaysariyyas, and with special places assigned for the main groups of craftsmen or traders. Fourthly, there would be a "core" of residential quarters, marked by at least two special characteristics: the combination of local with ethnic or religious differentiation, and the relative separateness and autonomy of each quarter or group of quarters. . . . Fifthly and finally, there would be the "suburbs" and outer quarters where recent and unstable immigrants would live and certain occupations be carried on: in particular the "caravan" quarters spread out along the main roads.*[23]

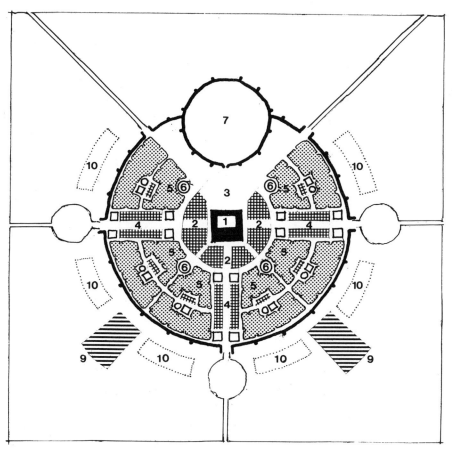

1. *Jami' Mosque* 2. *Specialized Markets or Suqs* 3. *Square or Maiydan* 4. *Suqs on the Thoroughfare with Khans at both ends* 5. *Residential quarters with their own mosque, market, and bath house* 6. *Hamam* 7. *Citadel with Government Complex* 8. *Walls & Gates* 9. *Cemetery* 10. *Semirural Districts*

FIGURE 2.5 A Schematic Plan of the Early Medieval Arab City, According to Ismail (1972).

This urban structure as described by Hourani, in addition to the earlier elements described by Von Grunebaum, completed the picture of a stereotype still used by many to discuss and teach the Muslim city of the pre-industrial era. The stereotype continued to be adopted by scholars from different disciplines working in different parts of the world.

For example, Nader Ardlan and Laila Bakhtiar, two Iranian architects, go the further step of attempting to relate that urban physical structure to a larger *zietgiest* in Islamic society.[24] Using the works of a number of Muslim sufi philosophers, Ardlan and Bakhtiar, writing in the early 1970s, constructed a graphic diagram of a typical Muslim city, but this time they also introduced the idea that the form of the Muslim city is analogous to the cosmic structure (FIGURE 2.6).

Within the city, the ideal Muslim, represented by the caliph, situates himself in a single point in space, creating the center of a spiritual exchange represented by the mosque. As the Muslim moves in space and time, so do his surroundings, establishing the line of the bazaar which contains all other buildings and which constitutes the center of earthly exchanges. The outside walls delimit the city as a form that symbolizes the cosmos, and finally the location of the gates recalls the cardinal orientations. Ardlan's and Bakhtiar's interpretation of physical form was not based on any structured historical research. Rather their views seem to stem from an experiential understanding of one of Islam's great cities, Isfahan, looked at using only one branch of Islamic philosophy, sufi mysticism. However, and in spite of the author's attempt to generate a model based on pure Islamic ideals, their diagram, if compared to the earlier ones we discussed, seems to have been influenced by the Von Grunebaumian stereotype. To their credit, Ardlan and Bakhitiar did not extend their argument to include cities other than those of Islamic Persia.

Heinz Gaube, who was also working on Iranian cities, took a different line from that of Ardlan and Bakhtiar.[25] Gaube, a German historian and archaeologist, was more concerned with the physical history of Iranian cities which, according to him, were a regional variation of the typical Islamic city.[26] Gaube's Islamic city had four major functions which manifested themselves in physical form: (1) governmental authority was represented by the palace or the citadel, (2) religious and intellectual life were embodied in the mosques and the *madrasas*, (3) economic exchange took place in the shops, *qaysariyas*, and caravansaries of the bazaar, and (4) urban population occupied the residential quarters. Gaube then proceeds to describe the form of the city:

> *The city walls, which with a few exceptions have a polygonal plan, contain a variable number of gates (A). Through some of these gates, overland roads enter the city. The most frequented of these overland roads run through the suburbs (B), where economic subcenters very often have been developed, generally near the gates. Within the city's walls, the overland roads continue as the main axes of intra-urban commu-*

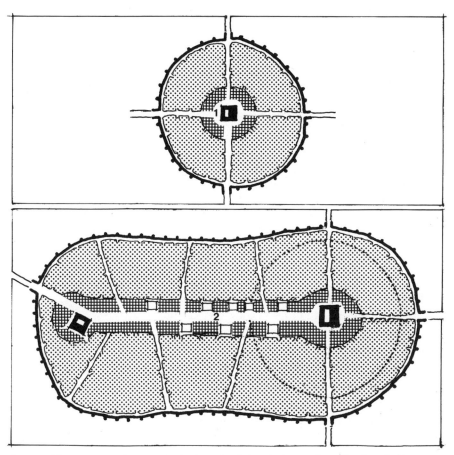

1. (TOP) Mosque as a stationary point in time simulating the human being (or the caliph) surrounded by the universe (or the city) 2. (BOTTOM) As the human being moves, so would the city, transforming a concentric concept into a linear one (in reality this is represented by the spinal bazaar)

FIGURE 2.6 The General Order of the Muslim City, According to Ardlan and Bakhtiar (1973).

nication. The Great Mosque is located on the main axis, or very near to it, and in many cases close to the center of the city. Near the mosque there are often administrative institutions, and at least one of the important madrasas *(C). . . . The center of the bazaar is at the place of the highest density of intraurban circulation, i.e., near the crossing of two or more axes. The bazaar (D) is the most distinctive characteristic*

> *of the Islamic city. [It] can develop linealy, that is, along the intraurban main-axes, or it can spread over the center of the city. In most cases we find a combination of both types. Behind the shops and workshops of the bazaar there are the caravansarais, the establishments of the long-distance and wholesale trade, the courtyards for the crafts and industry, warehouses, and offices(E). . . . The bazaar has no residential function at all. The living quarters are separated from it and are scattered over the whole city. (F)*[27]

This description and the accompanying diagram, which Gaube titled "The main elements of the Islamic city" (FIGURE 2.7), appear in the first chapter of his book on Iranian cities. Obviously, Gaube's description bears a great deal of resemblance to the stereotype, as identified by Von Grunebaum and elaborated on by Hourani. Because Gaube placed this discussion in the beginning of the book and because he made no attempt at any critical examination of it, we can conclude that his preceding analysis of the Muslim cities of Iran was mainly an attempt to study regional variations of the norm. In other words, Gaube was more interested in observing Iranian cities through the criteria of the stereotype instead of seeing Iranian cities in their own terms.

Gaube's book is a good example of the influence of the stereotype of Von Grunebaum and Hourani.

Another example may be found in the work of Samuel Noe, a planning historian. In an article entitled "In Search of the Traditional Islamic City", Noe, who deals with the city of Lahore, Pakistan, followed a more direct approach.[28] first, he adopted Hourani's six elements as given, then he embarked on a comparison between the traditional city of Lahore and the stereotypical Muslim city as identified by Von Grunebaum. All along, his main purpose was to relate cities from the Indian subcontinent to what he calls "the more extensive literature" on the traditional Islamic city. Noe's comparison of the features of Lahore with those of the stereotypical Muslim city revealed many similarities and a few minor differences.[29]

Again, Noe's article is an example of the effectiveness and power of the stereotypical model. Scholars working all over the Muslim world, as we have observed, were either using it to describe the cities they were researching or were searching for elements of it in the archaeology of urban existence. Scholars of the 1980s seem to have also been constricted by the stereotype. For example, J. Wagstaff, writing recently on the origin and evolution of towns in the Middle East,[30] sketched another diagrammatic model of the typical Muslim city (FIGURE 2.8). His model is not at all different from the ones I described earlier.

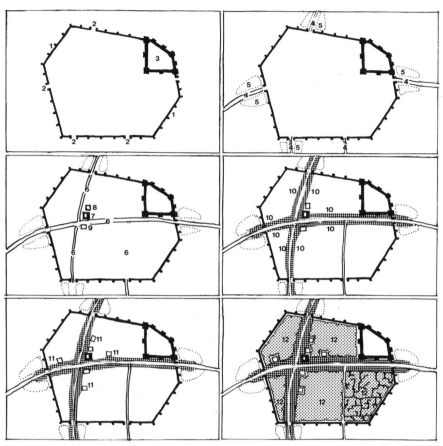

1. *City walls* 2. *City gates* 3. *Citadel* 4. *Overland roads* 5. *Suburbs* 6. *Urban thorough-fares* 7. *Great Mosque* 8. *Administrative Institutions* 9. *Madrasas* 10. *Bazaar* 11. *Cara-vanserais* 12. *Living Quarters*

FIGURE 2.7 Structure and Main Elements of the Islamic City with Concentration on Iran, According to Gaube (1979).

As sources for this diagram, Wagstaff cited, among others, Von Grunebaum, Ismail, and Hourani, and his diagram again bears a great deal of resemblance to the plan of medieval Cairo, especially with the water canal on the western side of the city, a situation almost unique to Cairo.

The latest elaboration on the stereotypical Muslim city may be found in the work of Besim Hakim. In a book titled *Arabic-Islamic Cities* but based only on a case study of the City of Tunis, Hakim attempted another identification of the typical elements of the Muslim city in a clear axonometric diagram.[31] In describing his elements, Hakim used statements by early Arab geographers, historians and jurists, yet if we check his sources we also find that he essentially relied on the classic articles by the Marcais brothers and Von Grunebaum from

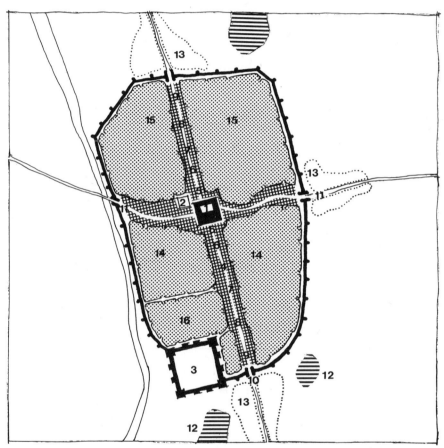

1. Friday Mosque 2. College (Madrasah) 3. Citadel 4. Bazaar 5. Candlemakers & Perfumers 6. Booksellers & Bookbinders 7. Leatherworkers & Shoemakers 8. Carpetmakers, Jewelers, & Tailors 9. Carpenters, Locksmiths, & Coppersmiths 10. Basketmakers, Saddlers, & Blacksmiths 11. Tanners & Potters 12. Cemeteries 13. Suburbs 14. Muslim Quarters 15. Christian Quarters 16. Jewish Quarters

FIGURE 2.8 Model of a Typical Islamic Town, According to Wagstaff (1983). (Compare to the plan of medieval Cairo in CHAPTER 5.)

the early decades of this century. In the book, Hakim convincingly argued that Islamic law was particularly responsible for giving the Muslim city its characteristic physical form. And although his conclusions are unique, his method may still allow us to place his work within the the cumulative chain of research that supports the stereotypical model.

It appears then that the stereotype seems to have evolved, developed, and matured as a result of cumulative research done by both occidental or western, and oriental or eastern scholars writing mainly in English and French. Here again we are reminded by the practice of *Isnad* or the chain of authority in Islam that seems to continue in contemporary scholarship. It is ironic that the Arab scholars working on the subject of the Muslim city chose not to contradict the existing authoritative body of literature produced by orientalists in spite of their awareness of some of its fallacies. It is even more ironic that they chose not to return to the early Arab sources but instead adopted many unproven notions nurtured by Westerners about the Muslim city. Their desire to gain legitimacy among their European peers led them to participate in the academic construction of a myth and the institutionalization of inaccurate knowledge on the Muslim city.

THE BROADER PICTURE: RESEARCH FROM OTHER DISCIPLINES

In general terms, a more accurate and less stereotyped view of the Muslim city can be drawn from work in different disciplines, scholarship that did not seek to understand it directly, but that instead analyzed the structures and institutions of Islamic society. To be able to unfold the typical Muslim city we have to extend our analysis beyond the work of those concerned with its form and situate ourselves within the larger framework of urban research and orientalist scholarship. We should note that the term *orientalist* here is not meant to be pejorative but is rather employed for its descriptive value.

The stages of development of the concepts of the Muslim city envisioned by researchers in a certain time is mainly the product of the state of scholarship and the predominance of particular research theories at that same point in time. Accordingly, we may be able to relate the stages of development of the stereotype to corresponding phases of orientalist scholarship.

For example, in the evolutionary stage, the Marcais brothers, Sauvaget, LeTourneau, and Berque were all concerned with identifying institutional elements (like the mosque, the bazaar, the bathhouse, etc.) so as to prove that Muslim cities were "real" cities too, like their medieval European counterparts. In doing so they must have been very influenced by the then fashionable Weberian notion of what makes a city. Max Weber had suggested in the later decades of the nineteenth century that there were five distinguishing marks of the medieval city: fortification, markets, a legal and administrative system, distinctive urban forms of association, and partial autonomy.[32] Since the Muslim town lacked some of these marks, Weber maintained that they were not cities. Furthermore, he argued that the city had fully existed only in medieval Europe but not in the Middle East. Weber's notions were very influential on all scholars of urban history at the turn of the twentieth century. His influence could be observed in the work of medievalists and orientalists alike. Weberian thought, coupled with the formalist tendencies of early orientalists, created an atmosphere that was conducive to the evolution of the first stereotype. The mosque, the market and the public baths identified by the Marcais brothers, all represented an attempt by the formalist tradition in orientalism to specify equivalent institutions to those of the medieval European city.

In defense of the Muslim city, several renowned scholars such as Massignon and Brunschvig engaged in investigations that contradicted Weber's criteria. Robert Brunschvig was one of the few early scholars who attempted to investigate the underlying causes of the physical pattern of Muslim cities.[33] His exploration led him to the conclusion that legal and religious bodies played an important institutional role in Muslim urban life. Using old Arabic manuscripts, Brunschvig demonstrated that Muslim law practiced by *qadis* or judges relating to urban problems yielded the physical fabric and urban structure of Muslim cities.

Massignon's work on "Sinf" also led him to the belief that a guild-like organization of professional cooperation was a predominant urban institution in the life of a Muslim city. Such organization, as Massignon believed, provided the basis of urban society in the Middle East and established the concept of social solidarity among the community of believers.[34] As we can see, Brunschvig, Massignon, and even Berque were unintentionally responding to Weber's contentions. They were all trying to prove that the Muslim city possessed similar or equivalent institutions to those of Europe.

As I mentioned earlier, it was under Von Grunebaum that the stereotype reached its maturity. As Janet Abu-Lughod had shown earlier, what Von Grunebaum did was very simple! First he combined the 1928–1945 work of the Marcais brothers on the Maghreb with the 1941 work of Sauvaget on the Mashreq and arrived at the physical form of the typical Muslim city. Then, he married this physical form to the institutional structure identified by Gibb, Massignon, Brunschvig, and others in the late 1940s. The result of this marriage was the stereotype.

Since Von Grunebaum's model did not represent elements or structures that may be found in all Muslim cities nor did it portray any one Muslim city in particular, it could be considered a total abstraction to the extent of being imaginary. This situation becomes much clearer if we look at the broader picture of Von Grunebaum's work, as Laroui[35] and Said[36] did. Laroui's analysis showed that, in general, Von Grunebaum employed A. L. Kroeber's culturalist theory to understand Islam. The application of this theory entailed a series of reductions and eliminations through which Islam was represented as a closed system of exclusions. As Said tells us:

> Von Grunebaum has fallen prey both to the orientalist dogmas he inherited and to the particular features of Islam which he has chosen to interpret. . . . Von Grunebaum's Islam, after all, is the Islam of the earlier European orientalists — monolithic, scornful of ordinary human experience, gross, reductive, unchanging. . .[37]

The net result of Von Grunebaum's work was a historical vision of a Muslim city interpreted by a theory of culture unequipped to include the true experiences of its own residents. The Muslim city to Von Grunebaum was thus a unitary phenomenon incapable of creative development or objective order, as can be seen in the following statement:

> The Islamic town did not represent a uniform type of civilized life as had the Greek or Roman town. . . deliberate imitation of a superior cultural standard [in the Muslim cities] does occur but is rare.[38]

Von Grunebaum's obvious dislike of Islam, once explained by Laroui and Said, again casts a more obscure context of his stereotype. This background should make us more aware that the evolution of the stereotype was not only influenced by the general tendencies in orientalist scholarship but also and to a greater degree by the political ideologies or personal biases of orientalist scholars.

By the 1960s, the Von Grunebaum stereotype had spread all over academic circles in the world and was adopted by scholars from east and west. For example, in his monumental work *The Venture of Islam*, Marshall Hodgson's discussion of urban order in Islamic civilization is based on the stereotype.[39]

What Hodgson achieved in his account was mainly a synthesis of the concept of the Muslim town as described physically by Von Grunebaum and socioculturally by Goiten and Lapidus.[40] Hodgson is, however, an exception because the adoption and the subsequent dissemination of the stereotype were not necessarily reflective of the general revisionist tendencies that dominated his era. Many of the early notions about Muslim urban life were now being critically revised. For example, Massignon's theory of Muslim guilds was challenged by Cahen who showed that such professional corporations were not guilds in the medieval European sense, but insofar as they existed were only instruments of state control.[41]

Goiten pointed out that there was no Arabic equivalent for the term *guild*. He suggested that there was no such word because there was no such institution.[42] More generally, Stern noticed that the absence of professional organizations is only one example of the absence of organizations in Islamic society.[43] Abdel-Rahim recognized that the absence of municipal autonomy and local self-government did not prevent cities from flourishing as great centers of commerce and culture in the Muslim world.[44]

Since Muslim cities were organized on bases other than those of municipal autonomy and local self-government characteristic of their European counterparts, it followed that the legal and administrative institutions of Muslim cities did not and could not have possessed a representative character as did medieval European municipalities. Anthropologists such as Eickelman placed critical emphasis on the notion of the quarter. He described it as a cluster of households characterized by a particular quality of social closeness that is based on multiple personal ties, common interests, and shared moral unity. He characterized the physical form of the quarter and the city in general as one that follows a cultural logic, not in terms of physical layout or visual landmarks but in regard to the conceptions of social order.[45] Finally, Cahen[46] and Aubin[47] demonstrated that many of the characteristics that we call "Islamic city" were in fact those of the medieval Italian city, the Byzantine city, or even the Asian or Chinese city.

This revisionist trend culminated in Ira Lapidus's classic *Muslim Cities in the Later Middle Ages*, which is justifiably critical of earlier research.[48] Instead of testing the proposition that the city did not fully exist in the Muslim Middle East, Lapidus reformulated the issue by asking the question what the forces were that established Muslim cities as functional urban entities in the Middle East. He concluded by suggesting that Muslim urban society was not an entity defined by any particular political or socioeconomic body but rather a society that divided essential powers and functions among its different component groups. This system of relations constituted the government of Muslim cities whose urban form was the outcome of interactions between these subsidiary groups.

Those groups, according to Lapidus, were the military elites, the *ullama* or religious leaders, the local notables and merchants, and the urban commoners. Lapidus's work represented the first attempt on the part of an orientalist to analyze the Muslim city in its own terms. For this reason we see little of the stereotype in his work. However, Lapidus's findings were not followed up on by the physicalist or those scholars concerned mainly with the physical form of the city.

Lapidus's identification of the subsidiary groups that made up Muslim urban life and his suggestion that the social organization of Muslim society was the main factor that contributed the most to giving the city its form were not as simple to grasp or as appealing as Hourani's stereotypical model discussed earlier.[49] The simplicity of Hourani's abstraction and the power of his generalizations paved the way for the adoption of the stereotype by scholars from a variety of fields and cultures, and it is precisely from that point that we may notice a split between the general tendencies of oriental scholars working mainly in the West, on one hand, and the particular interest of the physicalists working on other parts of the world, like India, Iran, and even Indonesia, on the other hand. So we can see that the consolidation of the stereotype took place in spite of the revisionist positions in orientalist scholarship and not because of it.

The situation got even more complicated in the 1970s and 1980s. With the publication of Edward Said's *Orientalism*, a new chapter in the study of the Muslim city was inadvertently opened.[50] In *Orientalism*, Said presented for the first time a study of the scholars who study the Muslim orient, their methods, their biases, and their influence in directing research orientation through their institutional power.

According to Said, an orientalist, whether an individual or an institution, has a certain idea or representation of the "orient" defined as being other than the "occident." To them, it is mysterious, unchanging, and ultimately inferior. By analyzing the work of the most established orientalists, like Gibb, Massignon, and Von Grunebaum, Said successfully identified the fallacies of orientalism as a field of research. We also learn from Said that the influence of the institutions, under whose sponsorship many of these orientalist constructs were introduced, was so strong to the extent that many oriental scholars interested in working on issues of Muslim civilization had to accept orientalism's definition of their own social reality.

The impact of Said's book could be felt on many aspects of orientalist scholarship. One of these was the initiation of a new wave of literature and the establishment of some new research directions in the study of Muslim cities. Although each of the groups that started these new directions had their own agendas, which were considerably different from one another, they all had one thing in common: their anti-orientalist stands. I classify these groups, according to the type of research they engaged in, into two distinct groups — the philosophical and the political-nationalist. It is worthwhile to note here that many scholars working in these groups had established positions before Said's book came out. However, without Said's ideas we could not have easily classified their work.

The philosophical group, which includes people like Ardlan, engaged in research that attempted to bring together the study of Muslim philosophy and Muslim urban and architectural form. Using Sufism, as one branch of Islamic religious and spiritual practice, to explore and interpret the form of the city was justified because it led to new levels of understanding urban form.[51] The centrality of the mosque and the royal quarters, for example, were getting a new interpretation. The early orientalist notions which considered their centrality a representation of manifest centralized authority was now being replaced, at least so far as the scholars of this group were concerned, with the idea that it was a product of latent spiritual belief related to the concept of oneness in Islam. Along these lines, other scholars in this group engaged in similar investigations that used Arabic language, literature, and mythology to interpret city form.[52] Although the work of this group has not yet yielded substantial results, it is still gaining momentum and there is no telling of where it could lead.

The second group is the political nationalist, whom I have termed such because they mostly are from very traditional Arab societies, because their research is mainly sponsored by countries with strong political ideologies or because their writing has a distinctive nationalist tone. Hakim, al-Hathloul, and Akbar are good representatives of this group.[53] The revisionist trend should have had an impact on those scholars. Some of them, however, discarded it because they saw that trend as an attack on the concept of the Muslim city and ultimately on their institutional legitimacy.

In defense of the concept of the Muslim city, many conferences were held in and outside the Muslim world. Among them, for example, were the conference on the Institutions of the Islamic City sponsored by UNESCO in 1980, the conference on Islamic Urbanism sponsored by the Saudi Arabian government in 1980, the conference on the Arab City sponsored by the Organization of Arab Towns in 1981, the conferences on Middle Eastern Cities in Comparative Perspective sponsored by the Franco-British research group in 1984 and 1986, and the conference on the Middle East City sponsored by the Professors for World Peace Association in 1987.[54] In the introduction to the proceedings of this last conference, the editor, A. Saggaf, identifies the general theme of the book by quoting a controversial paragraph from Lapidus:

> We can no longer think of Muslim cities as unique. . . . None of the characteristic bodies of Muslim society were specifically urban forms of organization. . . . Cities were physical entities but not unified social bodies defined by characteristically Muslim qualities.[55]

Saggaf then follows this up with his own response:

> Of course, most scholars take issue with Professor Lapidus since Muslim cities do have certain distinctive features. They have a unique layout and physical design, the central focus point of which is always a Maidan around a castle or palace on one hand and the central mosque on the other hand.[56]

Obviously Saggaf's response is an excellent example of the reactionary tendencies of the nationalist scholars. It is ironic that in reaction to Lapidus's revisionist view, which Saggaf understood as an attack on the concept of the Muslim city he reverts to the stereotypical model of Von Grunebaum that we have demonstrated to be the source of most problems. It is as if to defend the concept of the Muslim city, it was now legitimate to use the work of the orientalist who introduced it, even though much of the orientalist assumptions were proven wrong.

The work of Hakim and al-Hathloul, though scholarly, seems to have been motivated by these nationalist tendencies. In his introduction, Hakim told us that he believes that there is an Islamic reason behind the form or Arab Muslim cities. He argued that Islamic law has been particularly responsible for the cellular pattern of the Muslim city. Citing *fatawi* or rulings by Malki jurists rendered to resolve urban and building disputes, Hakim identified how window and door locations, building heights and functional uses were determined and how these factors influenced the shape of the Muslim city. He then went on to identify thirteen different elements from which Muslim cities were made. In his conclusion, Hakim suggested that the earlier reliance on Islam as a basis for analyzing Muslim cities was essentially sound. He also suggested that his work revealed that the roots of the form of all Muslim cities could primarily be attributed to the building principles that were generated by Islamic divine law. In his words:

> *Hence, all cities in the Arab and Islamic world inhabited by Muslims share an Islamic identity which is directly due to the application of Sharia values in the process of city building.*[57]

By attributing the entire form of the city to one single factor and by generating static typical physical elements for the city, this determinist and formalist work falls into the old orientalist trap.

Here we can clearly see a split in the broader picture. At a time when the revisionist and anti-orientalist literature was changing our basic assumptions about Muslim cities, the stereotypical model was still held dearly by many of the formalists who could not see beyond the immediate physical qualities of cities.

With this we come to the conclusion of this part. I believe that we have demonstrated that the stereotypical Muslim city form was constructed by a series of western authorities who drew upon a small sample of cities from a variety of locations. The development of the stereotype then accompanied the development of orientalist scholarship. Subsequently, the stereotype that was invented by westerners was adopted by some Arab and Muslim scholars who for political and nationalistic reasons became its main advocates. No one could summarize this state of affairs better than Edward Said:

> *No scholar or school is a perfect representative of some ideal type or school in which by virtue of national origin or the accidents of history, he participates. Yet in so relatively insulated and specialized a tradition as orientalism. . . there is in each scholar some awareness, partially conscious and partly unconscious, of national tradition, if not national ideology.*[58]

I have tried to show how the attempts to understand and describe the Muslim city were severely affected by the biases and beliefs of both early and late scholars. Norman Daniels has pointed out some constraints acting upon the early scholars who were Christian thinkers. The most important of these was their attempt to understand Islam analogically by seeing Muhamed as the

Christ of the Muslims. This resulted in the polemic title "Mohammedism."[59] Out of all these misconceptions Islam became an image whose function was not so much to represent Islam in itself as to present it for the medieval Christian. The stereotype was only a component example of this broader image, and instead of observing the unique conditions of particular cities, cities were adapted to fit the stereotype.

In this chapter I have presented a brief historiography of the concept of the Muslim city. I have also attempted to raise a whole set of questions relevant to a discussion of Muslim city form: How does one represent cities? What is city form? Is the notion of a distinct city based on religion a useful one? How do concepts and ideas acquire legitimacy, and how do scholars acquire authority? Although I have not fully answered these questions, my goal has been partially achieved. My intention has been to examine a particular system of ideas and a network of concepts and not, by any means, to displace them with new ones. This present network of concepts does not seem to work any more and it ought to be replaced not by an alternative "objective" network but by an interdisciplinary analysis of intentions of the makers and the actions of the inhabitants over a reasonable period of time. We should let Muslim cities define their own system of relationships, symbolic languages, and metaphoric messages.

This may only be possible if we give some attention to the early Arabs who went about establishing one of the world's greatest cultural traditions. We need to know more about these early Arabs, about the urban images they brought with them from Arabia, about the urban settings they conquered from those they called "infidels," and about the gradual process of change and transformation that ensued. We may find some answers if we look into what the Muslims originally wanted of their cities and try to relate that to what Muslim cities turned out to be. We may also find some answers if we look at the cities of "Dar Al-Islam" or the cities of the new Islamic tradition, a task that will be taken on later. In this chapter I have argued against something and not for something else. I have thus told half a story; the other half is an entirely different story in itself.

III

URBAN CREATIONS OF THE EARLY MUSLIM ARABS
THE GARRISON TOWN AS A PROTOTYPE

Arabia constituted an almost perfect architectural vacuum and the term 'Arab' should never be used to designate the architecture of Islam.[1]

K.A.C. CRESWELL

Until recently, the view that the architecture of the early Muslim Arabs was not worthy of study because it was "primitive" has dominated the field of Islamic architectural history. Of course, from a nationalistic standpoint, this situation has represented the ethnocentricity of western scholars studying Muslim environments. Creswell, like many of the other orientalists, was heavily biased from the outset. After all, he was a soldier in the British colonial army. Since the vernacular architecture of the Arabian Peninsula in pre-Islamic times has never been adequately studied, one can take issue with Creswell's sweeping generalization.

The issue of whether or not Arabia constituted an architectural vacuum before the advent of Islam is central to any discussion of Muslim cities. If we accept Creswell's view, it follows that the urban creations of the early Muslims should not be designated as "Arab" too. Having treated this issue in his *Formation of Islamic Art*, Grabar concluded that a series of factors in the ninth century brought about the "classical" moment that started a unique Islamic art created for Arab purposes.[2] Again, whether Grabar's argument applies to cities is an issue that remains to be seen. It is my intention in this chapter to explore this topic further by investigating the relationship between the initial urban intentions of the early Muslim Arabs and the physical forms they actually created.

From the discussion in the previous chapter, we know the general components of the stereotypical Muslim city. This city had a central mosque, a central open space, a bazaar extending out of the mosque into the main thoroughfare, and a circulation system branching off into the cul-de-sacs that serviced the segregated residential quarters. Earlier I showed that this description was arrived at through accumulation and that it probably represents a mental image of a nonexisting physical reality. The question that this chapter poses is how different those early Arab towns were from the stereotype.

To start, we go back to the time of the early conquest and look back at the circumstances that surrounded the Arabs' earliest urban creations. Out of the wilderness of the desert and from a small town called Mecca started the story of Islam. Its prophet Muhamad, born to a culture of pagan belief, called for the worship of one God. His fundamental teachings included that man must submit to God and fear his final day of judgement. He assigned his followers five main religious duties. Those were the *shehadah*, or proclamation of the oneness of God and the prophecy of Muhamad; *salah*, which were five daily prayers; *siam*, or the fasting of the Arabic month of Ramadhan; *zakah*, which implied the giving of alms; and *hajj*, or the pilgrimage to Mecca for those who could afford it.

The Mohamadan call established a stronghold over its Arab followers, and to spread the word of Islam, the Arabs went about invading far places and lands of other races. They started first by unifying themselves in the Arabian Peninsula. This was achieved while Muhamad was alive. After his death, he was succeeded by the four orthodox caliphs: Abu Bakr (11/632–13/634), 'Umar (13/634–23/644), 'Uthman (23/644–35/656), and 'Ali (35/656–40/661).

Here it may be important for us to review the forces that started the conquest and the factors that led to its success. For this, we will primarily refer to the work of Fred Donner.[3] Donner suggested several causes for the conquest, among which were: the ideological nature of the Islamic religion, which convinced the Arabs that they had an essentially religious duty to expand and fulfill a divinely ordained mission; the desire on the part of the ruling elite to expand the political boundaries of the new state in order to secure even more fully the trans-Arabian commerce; the possibility that members of the elite saw an expansion of the state as necessary in order to preserve their positions at the top of the new political hierarchy; and the declining productivity of the Arabian Peninsula and its inability to cope with the increased population, which lead to a cycle of attacks on neighboring territories.

Building on the work of others, Donner also suggested some factors that may have led to the tremendous success of the Islamic conquest. Among these were the weaknesses that the Byzantine and Sassanian empires were undergoing at the time due to prolonged warfare, the destruction caused by the immense floods in Southern Iraq before the conquest, the disaffection of many of the subjects of the two empires, the convenience of inner lines of communication that the Muslims enjoyed, and the remarkable degree to which the new Islamic state with its expansionist policy could harness for its purposes the rugged warriors of Arabia.

Whether we accept Belyaev's Marxist interpretation of the causes of the conquest or Von Grunebaum's explanation of the mood of the times that led to its success, we must recognize that the conquest was primarily an Arab Muslim movement.[4] Although "Islam" was one factor among many, we must accept that it was the main drive behind the conquest.[5] It was Islam that finally sparked the whole integration process and welded into an incredibly effective fighting force those tribes whose energies had been consumed by petty quarrels among themselves.[6]

> *The success of the conquest was, then, first and foremost the product of an organizational breakthrough of proportions seldom paralleled in the history of Arabian Society.*[7]

The success of the conquest brought about the need to establish defensive posts to define the territory of the new empire. Indeed, it is generally agreed that the new garrison towns seem to have been primarily established to control the non-Arab populations of the conquered domains, to defend Arabia from invasion by either the Byzantines or the Sassanians, and to function as the springboards for further campaigns.[8]

Garrison towns were of two main types. Some, like Kufah in Iraq, Fustat in Egypt, and Qairawan in Tunisia, were *Fustats*, or mass encampments of makeshift tent settlements that in time grew into permanent cities as Arab immigration to them was encouraged. Others, like Rabat in Morocco and Monastir in Tunisia, were *Ribats*, or border garrisons that grew into fortress towns and became the nuclei of important cities.[9] A few garrisons were placed in existing towns. The term *Amsar* (Arabic sing: *mesr*, or *misr*) was later used during the reign of the second orthodox Caliph 'Umar (13/634–23/644) to designate those *fustats* and *ribats* that were selected as centers to manage the conquered territories and as bases from which further military campaigns could be launched.[10]

The *amsar* played a very important role in the political development of the Islamic state during the first Hijri century. In fact, it would not be an exaggeration to say that the chronicled history of that century is primarily a history of the *amsar*.[11] In Iraq, Basrah and Kufah were the first garrison towns to be designated as *amsar*[12] (FIGURE 3.1).

BASRAH: THE FIRST GARRISON TOWN (13/634)

The site where Basrah was built was known to the local inhabitants in pre-Islamic times. The desert area west of the site was probably used as the famous Jahilia *suq*, or market called *Marbad*.[13] Musawi, studying the relationship between the Arabs and the Persians in this area, suggested that the market was intentionally placed in this somewhat desolate location by the Persian administration. Their main objective was to reduce the friction between the Arabs and Persians residing in an area with ill-defined borders.[14]

The first major confrontation between the Arabs and the Persians in this region was at nearby Ubbla. The success of the Muslim armies in Ubbla and especially at the Battle of Dhi Qar encouraged the Arab tribes living in the region to start their intermittent raids on the western borders of the ailing Sassanian empire. Although the raids were scattered and unorganized, Caliph 'Umar seized this opportunity to consolidate the Arab tribes into the Muslim army under the command of Sa'ad ibn abi-Waqas.[15] The army was put in charge of expanding the territory of Islam into Persian land. The fighting, which lasted three years, brought a lot of Arabs from the mainland. 'Utba ibn Ghazuan was named to lead this new garrison that was primarily responsible for the conquest of the southwestern cities of the Sassanian Empire. The conquest was relatively successful, and the Arabs started to settle in and around the newly conquered area.

Feeling somewhat cut off from the rest of Arabia, the newly settled garrison started to make demands on the caliph to declare any of the places they settled a *Mesr*. This is evident from Utba's letter to Caliph 'Umar that stated: "The Muslim troops are in need of a place to return to and reside when they are not in battle."[16]

The caliph initially refused because all the sites that the Arabs were considering were east of the Euphrates. Instead, he responded with the famous letter in which he ordered: "Do not settle in a place where you would be separated from your Caliph by a river or any water barrier."[17] 'Umar further requested that the Arabs identify a nearby place west of the river to which they could move. The site of the close-by and abandoned *Marbad* market was thus an appropriate alternative.

Accordingly, the Arabs first settled the site of Basrah as a camp from which they could start their military campaigns against the Sassanians. Al-Baladhri and Yaqut actually tell us that it was the success of the ensuing invasions that helped populate Basrah.[18] News of such successes were reaching back home in the heart of Arabia, and hundreds of Arabs mainly from the tribes of Tamem and Bakr were emigrating to Basrah.

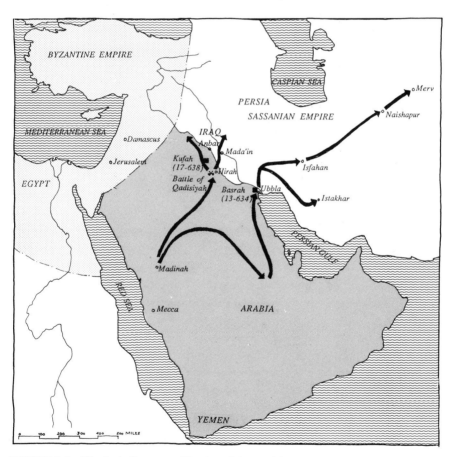

FIGURE 3.1   The Arab Conquest of Persia and the Establishment of Basrah and Kufah (13/634–17/638).

As the needs of the conquest grew, so did Basrah. Since it started as a military camp, its origins were very modest. A place for prayer and a residence of the army chief were laid out first, and around them the different tribes spread their tents, each in a given location.[19] Little is known about the nature and physical organization of these elements on site. Most scholars, however, assumed that the prayer place and the army chief residence must have occupied the center of the settlement as they were surrounded by tents from all sides.

The prayer place, which was simply a marked-out space, was assumed to be a mosque, although references to it as a *Masjid* do not appear in the chronicles until a later date. Similarly, the term *Dar al-Imarah*, meaning "the house of the *Amir*" or "governor," was used by most scholars to describe the residence of the army chief, although the chronicles do not provide any account of it as an actual building, at least in the initial stage. In fact, it took the Arabs a few months to embark on the construction of these buildings as temporary structures of reeds and canes. Baladhri informs us that the Arabs dismantled the reeds that made up these buildings and stored them when they left for a conquest. On their return they would reassemble the structure again.[20] This was the initial core of Basrah, a military camp for the early Mujahedin.

After the first few years, the Arabs started to realize that their situation in Basrah was becoming more permanent. They sent for their wives and families in Arabia.[21] The ensuing shift in the social structure of the community, from fighting soldiers to extended families, was also accompanied by a shift in the materials employed in building: from the lightweight and temporary reeds to the heavier, more permanent mud bricks. The use of a more permanent material did not initially receive the approval of Caliph 'Umar. Jahez relates that it was with great reluctance that the caliph acknowledged the practice and advised, "I detest your doing so, but if you should, then build thicker walls and tighter roofs."[22]

The incident that followed the death of 'Utbah, the first governor of Basrah in 17/638, is of significance in understanding the early urban history of the city. 'Utbah had embarked on his pilgrimage early in the year and had appointed Mujasha'a ibn Mas'ud as acting governor. On his way to Mecca 'Utbah died, leaving Mujasha'a as the Amir of Basrah. This latter was, however, quickly replaced by the al-Mughirah ibn Shu'bah. The chronicles give conflicting accounts of this important incident. Some insist that the caliph appointed al-Mughirah upon hearing of 'Utbah's death. Others indicate that the residents of Basrah selected al-Mughirah as one of their own, thus putting into effect the important Islamic legal and political concept of *Shura*, or shared concerns. Regardless of who was in charge of appointing or electing al-Mughirah, most accounts agree that al-Mughirah was favored over Mujash'a because the former was an urbanite from Taif, while the latter was a bedwin probably unaccustomed to urban living and incapable of urban administration.[23]

Al-Mughirah did not last in office more than a year, and it was during the administration of his successor, Abu Musa al-'Ashri (17/638–29/649), that the actual development of Basrah took place. By the time Basrah was turned over to Abu Musa, a Madinese directly appointed by Caliph 'Umar, tribal conflicts and internal disputes had reached a peak.[24] In an attempt to resolve some of these conflicts and disputes, Abu Musa set out to reorganize the physical form of the settlement through a series of decisions on the urban functions of the town, which we might today call a redevelopment based on a new zoning plan. 'Abu-Musa seems to have achieved this through the use of the concept of *khutat* or *khitat* (Arabic sing. *Khutah* or *khitah*). *Khutat* were primarily plans marked out on the land.[25] Their use as a planning idea deserves some elaboration.

Abu Musa issued a *Khutah* to every tribe designating the areas in which they could build.[26] Abu Musa also paid attention to Basrah's surrounding hinterland. Land fit for agricultural use was distributed to tribal leaders who wanted it. Agricultural development was encouraged by the granting of waste land to potential developers. In historical and legal tradition, the prototype for this kind of an estate grant, *qatai'a*, was Caliph 'Umar's concession of some unused land on the periphery of Basrah to a man named Nafi, who had requested the land for the purpose of raising horses. Subsequently, *qatai'a* were given to army generals and tribal chiefs. Many of Basrah's residents either owned *qatai'a* or worked on them, and the size of such a *qatai'a* seems to have been generally reflective of the power or role of those who owned them.[27]

In fact, the demand for land, whether for residential or agricultural use, was so great that the caliph expressed some concern over the Arabs' sudden interest in acquiring property. Jahez related that the caliph sent a letter to the residents of Basrah, which stated, "Do not overutilize the land because it is full of fat!"[28]

According to al-Baladhri, the first *Khutat* planned in Basrah were the mosque and the Dar al-Imarah, which was originally located at some distance from the mosque. It was not until thirty years later, during the administration of Ziad (35/656–53/675), under the first Ummayad caliph, that the Dar al-Imarah was moved to the *qibla* side of the mosque.[29] The *suq*, or the market of Basrah, was also initially located at the Marbad Sahah, on the west side of the city. The new canal dug under the administration of Abd Allah ibn 'Amer (29/650–35/656) on the east side of the city seems to have changed the location of some of its economic activity. And soon the *suq* at Marbad withered and was replaced by another on the eastern side.[30] The chronicles make no reference to any market outside the mosque of Basrah in those early days, although we know that Caliph 'Umar had allowed street vendors to spread their goods in the equivalent space outside of the mosque in Madinah.[31] This situation seems to have been replicated in some of the *Amsar*, but not in Basrah, especially during its early years.

This initial arrangement of elements in Basrah is of significance because it indicates that the Arabs were not intent on any particular layout for the city. In fact, this scattered arrangement describes a plan that has no correlation to the stereotypical Muslim city where all these important functions — the mosque, the governor's residence and the market — occupy the center of the city. FIGURE 3.2 shows a schematic plan of Basrah following the first few years of its establishment.

The process of laying out Basrah is also of major significance because it informs us of the planning concerns of the early Arab settlers. According to al-

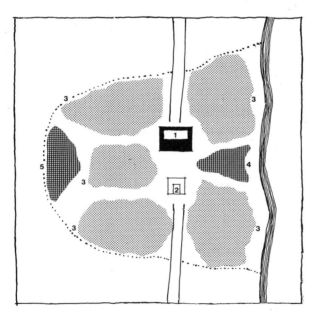

1. *Mosque*
2. *Dar al-Imarah*
3. *Residential quarters (Khutat)*
4. *Eastern Market*
5. *Suq al-Marbad*

FIGURE 3.2 The Early Organization of Basrah (13/634).

Mawardi, Basrah was divided into five sections containing individual *khutats* which were each assigned to a tribe.[32] The settlers made the width of its main street sixty cubits (a cubit is equal to 18 inches or 45 cm.), and this central spine served as a *marbad* or a kind of waystation. The other streets that separated the different sections of the settlement had a width of twenty cubits and these in turn branched off into the narrower seven-cubit lanes. In the middle of each *khutah* the settlers provided a wide *rahbah*, or square, where they could pray, meet, station their horses, and bury their dead.

Al-Baladhri further relates that the settlers within each khutat subdivided the land and built manazel, or houses that abutted each other.[33] This could have only happened at a later date when the administration of Abu Musa allowed the settlers to build permanent structures. **FIGURES 3.3** and **3.4** show a schematic configuration of the city thirty years after its establishment, following the development plans of Abu Musa and the redevelopment plans of Ziad.

It is doubtful that this initial form was a result of any specific Islamic principles or any particular planning ideology. There are also several aspects of this form or plan arrangement that can mislead us in our attempt to understand their value. For example, the spaces between the *khutat*, referred to in the Chronicles as *Turuq* or passways, were primarily intended to serve as barriers between the *khutat* and not necessarily as streets for movement or circulation. That they ended up being used as the major thoroughfares of Basrah was mainly a by-product of their function as a space separating feuding tribes.

The issue of who decided on the form of Basrah and how agreement on this form was reached is also of importance in our attempt to understand the genesis of the Arab-Muslim town. Since the *Amirs*, or governors, were mainly appointed by the caliph in Madinah, it could be assumed that the plans they implemented were representative of caliphal authority. But Akbar disagrees with this view. He suggests that the settlers themselves may have been in charge of the *Ikhtat*, a term designating the entire planning and building process.[34] Akbar bases this on al-Mawardi's statement that "people marked out the land and built their dwellings."[35]

Akbar concludes that since there was no mention of any authoritative figure, then the inhabitants of Basrah should be primarily credited with its planning. If we agree with his position, we may then conclude that the physical form of early Basrah was a reflection of the Islamic concept of *shura* which dictated a degree of shared power among all the Arab tribes who settled the city. The centrality of the mosque, the later movement of Dar al-Imarah to its side,

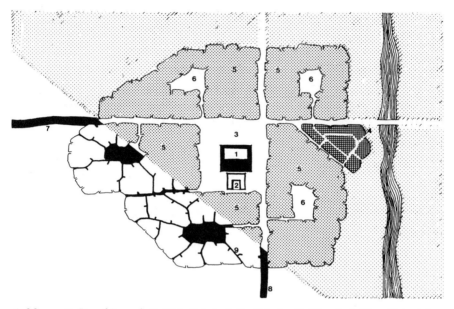

1. Mosque 2. Dar al-Imarah 3. Main Sahah 4. Suq/Market 5. Khutah 6. Khutah's burial grounds & prayer place 7. Main Thoroughfare (60 cubits) 8. Main Streets (20 cubits) 9. Lanes (7 cubits)

FIGURE 3.3   A Reconstruction of the General Organization of Basrah Following the Redevelopment Plan of 'Abu Musa and Ziad. (Around 53/675)

and even the layout of the entire city, may appear as less-significant factors in our attempt to understand the actual intention of the early Arab builders.

Setting aside the tribal settlement pattern that has been extensively discussed by Massignon, the form of the individual *khutat*, which we unfortunately know very little about, may play a more significant role in revealing the nature of the planning process that shaped early Basrah. In its early years Basrah seems to have been a scattered collection of different neighborhoods, each with its own center. The city started to take shape following the redevelopment efforts of Abu Musa and Ziad. The movement of Dar al-Imarah to the side of the mosque, the reconstruction of the mosque using permanent material, and the consolidation of the market area bordering the eastern canal provided the nucleus for Basrah's further growth and gave the city its first formal definition.

Finally, it is important for us to remember that the urban institutions of Basrah were not fully developed at the time its physical form was undergoing

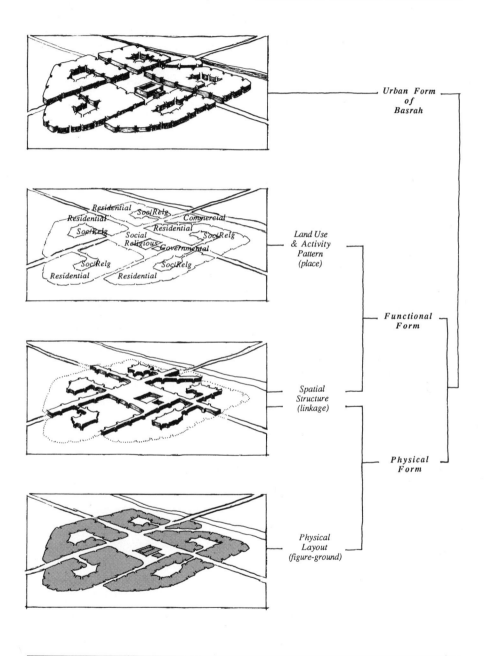

FIGURE 3.4 Basrah's Urban Form Analyzed.

its most drastic reorganization. Accordingly, the physical form of early Basrah may not serve as an adequate representation of its urban institutional structure. Instead, it stands as a still photograph documenting one stage in the development of a typical Muslim city.

THE IDEA OF DAR AL-HEJRAH

The fighting between the Arabs and the Persians finally ended with the Arabs' victory at the battle of Qadisiyah (15/637). The soldiers of Basrah were among those that participated in the battle. The Arab victory was consummated with the occupation of the Sassanian capital al-Mada'n.[36] Since the conquering forces were getting deeper into enemy territory, and since their role was changing from that of soldiers to that of settlers, the need for other new settlements like Basrah was becoming critical (refer to **FIGURE 3.1**).

The first recognition of this need was acknowledged Caliph 'Umar, who in a letter to his army chief Sa'ad suggested that "the Muslims should identify for themselves a *Dar Hejrah* and a *Qairawan*."[37] Literally translated *Dar al-Hejrah* means a "house for immigration," while *Qairawan* means "a pleasure place." The caliph's words were the first indication that he was willing and possibly interested in designating a place to which Arabs could immigrate and settle.

It is important to note that Caliph 'Umar did not ask Sa'ad to choose a *Mesr*, but instead he specified a *Dar al-Hejrah*! The difference here is very important because it may reveal much about the urban intentions of the early Arabs. *Dar al-Hejrah* served the religious needs of Islam by populating conquered land with Muslim residents. The designation of a place as a *Mesr* fulfilled the requirement of administering new territory. *Dar al-Hejrah* represented symbolic intentions while a *Mesr* represented administrative necessity. The Arabs, at least in this early stage, were not interested in building cities for the sake of what cities had to offer in return. Their main interest was in consolidating the gains of Islam, and at times this required the introduction of concepts like *Dar al-Hejrah* and *Mesr*. From this we can conclude that an urban place became a *Mesr* when it acquired an important economic, political, or defensive role for itself within the urban hierarchy of the Islamic empire. Its designation as *Dar al-Hejrah* was usually an essential earlier step in its development as a Muslim town, although this evolutionary relationship does not apply to all cases. Both Basrah and

Kufah must have served as symbolic *Dar Hejrah* before being declared administrative *Amsar*.

KUFAH: THE SECOND MESR (17/638)

Since the Arab army had just occupied and settled Ctesephon or Al-Mada'n, Caliph 'Umar's request that the Arabs designate a place for themselves to settle down was interpreted by Army chief Sa'ad as a caliphal approval of the new status of al Mada'n as a *Dar Hejrah*. But life in al-Mada'n was not easy for the Arabs. Ibn Khiyat reports that "its humid weather weakened their bodies and discolored their skin."[38]

Al-Baladhri further relates that the Arabs were frequently attacked by insects from the nearby river.[39] When the Caliph became aware of this situation, he sent a letter to Sa'ad that contained the following well-known request:

> *The Arabs are like camels, what is good for camels is good for them too.*
> *So move them out of the infested place and settle them in a desert site*
> *where no water can separate me from them.*[40]

Knowing of 'Umar's previous record regarding similar situations in Basrah, it seems that his decision was not only motivated by his concern for the public health of his soldiers but also by his desire to separate his soldiers from the local population of the conquered territories.[41]

It took Sa'ad a few months to locate a new site that would satisfy the caliph's criteria. This was the site of Kufah, and the Arabs started to spread their tents.[42] Since they were not at war at the time, Sa'ad soon realized that it was not realistic to ask the Arabs, who had just recently experienced the pleasures of urban living in Ctesephon and the like, to continue to live in tents. When Sa'ad sent to ask Caliph 'Umar's permission to build more-permanent structures, Umar replied:

> *The tents and camp life are more useful to your men than your walls and*
> *healthier to their bodies than your roofs. But I hate to forbid you, so if*
> *you build, build in reed.*[43]

The caliph, based on his expressed view regarding the above incidents, seems to have been against the idea of the Arabs' settling in already existing towns. He must have felt that mingling with the local population, enjoying the luxuries and comfort of urban living, and feeling a sense of permanence were factors that would subdue the Arab's fighting spirit.

We may add to these incidents a third one that would clearly demonstrate Umar's anti-urban and anti-building intentions. Two years after its establishment, Kufah underwent a serious fire resulting in the destruction of more than 80 reed-built houses.[44] The settlers then decided to rebuild those houses of mud and baked bricks. Sa'ad, fearing a caliphal veto, decided to write to 'Umar and consult him regarding the matter. Since Sa'ad himself was supportive of the peoples' decision, he decided to exert pressure on the caliph by sending a delegation of well-known residents of Kufah to seek caliphal advice and consent.[45] Under the circumstances it was difficult for 'Umar to deny them such permission. Reluctantly agreeing to their demand, the Caliph ordered them:

> Do not build high and do not build much. Do not build more than three houses each. Abide by the prophet's tradition and the state will be obliged to respect your practices.[46]

As for the physical form of the city, Sa'ad charged the responsibility of laying out the town to a man named Abu al-Haiyaj. This latter operated under terms established by the caliph. The streets were initially laid out to form a grid of major and minor thoroughfares and between them were the different *khutats*. The way that the different *khutats* were arranged seem to have been influenced by the desire to preserve the unified residence of all members of a given tribe. Abu al-Haiyaj, in fact, deserves the title of the "first Islamic city planner." In addition to helping out in drawing the original plan, Abu al-Haiyaj was also put in charge of establishing general settlement policy and resettling the *rauadef*, or the later immigrants. In order to make their transition to the city smoother, he established a *manakh*, or a reception station, for newly arriving tribesmen, in which they could live until they could be assigned an appropriate tract.[47]

The planning process seems to have been a very democratic one. Initially Sa'ad designated a group of residents as *Ahl al-Ra'i*, a kind of appraisal committee formed of men who had distinguished knowledge and opinion.[48] This group would get together to discuss options of division and estimation. Whenever they agreed on a course of action, their recommendations were forwarded to Abu al-Haiyaj, who in turn would issue the orders for land preparation and implement the decisions of land subdivisions.[49]

Al-Baladhri relates that the first space to be marked out was the mosque. The story has it that when Sa'ad arrived at the would-be site of the mosque, he ordered one of his soldiers to shoot an arrow toward the *qibla* in Mecca. Sa'ad then asked the archer to point three other arrows toward the opposite directions. The points where those arrows landed formed a square space at the center of which the mosque was built.[50] Al-Tabari concurs with al-Baladhri regarding the authenticity of this story, but he reverses the order of events. According to al-Tabari, the first *khutah* to be marked out on the land was the mosque. This was then followed by the marking out of a square platform around the mosque which al-Tabari calls *sahn*.[51] On the *qibla* side of the *sahn*, Sa'ad marked out his *dar*, or residence. It is interesting to note here that this residence which was initially marked out as Dar Sa'ad became later the Dar al-Imarah. This clearly indicates that Sa'ad was mainly laying out a house for himself as an army chief, without the awareness that he was deciding the location of the seat of government in the city of Kufah for years to come.

Another story of significance here is the one told by al-Tabari on the location of *Bait al-Mal*, or the public treasury. *Bait al-Mal* was initially part of Dar al-Imarah. One night, thieves broke in through a hole in the wall and stole some money. When Sa'ad consulted with Caliph 'Umar about this incident, the caliph asked him to move the mosque closer to his house and place it adjacent to it so that the side of the mosque facing the *qibla* would also be facing Dar al-Imarah (**FIGURE 3.5**). 'Umar's exact logic was that "the mosque is inhabited by day and by night and its people are the best guardians of their money."[52]

Sa'ad seems to have initially implemented the caliph's suggestion, but al-Tabari further reports a third stage in this development whereby a Persian resident of Kufah suggested an enlargement of the mosque following its relocation and proposed to Sa'ad to rebuild one large building as a "mosque and palace" instead. This also seems to have been achieved using stone from the ruins of a nearby Sassanian palace.[53]

These incidents, the archer shooting arrows and the burglary, were the main reasons that lead Creswell to conclude that the relationship between the mosque and Dar al-Imarah that persisted for more than two centuries was derived from two trivial facts.[54] Although this is probably true, it is important for us to analyze these incidents properly to understand the urban form of early Kufah. 'Umar's suggestion that the mosque be shifted to the side of Dar al-Imarah instead of vice versa does not imply that Dar al-Imarah was more important or central as a building type. His suggestion was based on the simple recognition that it would be easier to move or relocate the mosque because it was mainly a space and not a building. The mosque was a large yard delineated from two sides with a ditch to ensure that it would not be intruded upon by the surrounding buildings (Refer to FIGURE 3.5). Moving the mosque appears to have been a very simple operation since the colonnade was the only structure that needed to be reassembled in the new location.[55]

The *suq* or market of Kufah was located in the *Sahah*, or the square outside the mosque. Al-Tabari relates that the square preserved its form during the reign of 'Umar with Dar Sa'ad and the mosque as the only buildings.[56] Al-Ya'aqubi also reports that the market area of Kufah had no buildings or even roofs except for temporary shades erected by the sellers every day at their scattered locations.[57] It appears that the market of Kufah was not composed of any buildings and that it was primarily made of street vendors displaying their goods during the day then packing their stuff and leaving at the end of the day. This situation is easy to understand in light of 'Umar's position regarding the location of markets in Madina and the other Amsar. It is believed that 'Umar said:

> *Markets are to follow the tradition of mosques; whoever proceeds to a space, that space becomes his until he leaves it to home or finishes what he is selling.*[58]

Regarding the overall street structure of Kufah, al-Tabari relates that five main streets, or what he calls *manahej* (Arabic sing. *manhej*) were laid out north of the *sahah*. Four other streets were laid out to the south and three more to both east and west sides. All streets were supposedly parallel to this initial square core. The main *manahej* were 40 cubits wide. These, in turn, serviced side streets 20 cubits wide (9 meters or 30 feet) and a labyrinth of *zuqaqs* or narrow lanes that were 7 cubits (3 meters or 10 feet) wide.[59]

Based on the descriptions of al-Tabari and al-Ya'aqubi, Massignon provided us with the first attempt at a schematic organization of Kufah[60] (FIGURE 3.6). Using the same sources, al-Janabi completed the task and reconstructed the plans of the city as a very regular grid-iron[61] (FIGURE 3.7). Al-Janabi's plan represents some of the most recent research on the early form of Kufah. The few scholars who criticized it based their criticism on the fact that the plan was too orthogonal for a Muslim city, especially because it did not match the plan of Massignon.[62] The plan of Kufah as envisioned by al-Janabi should be looked upon as a schematic plan of what it was intended to be, and, as such, it still provides us with a lot of valuable information. In fact, we may be able to add on or modify al-Janabi's plan with additional details from various chronicles.

For example, al-Tabari relates that the tribes were assigned *khutats* that were located between the marked-out roads. He identified those tribes and the loca-

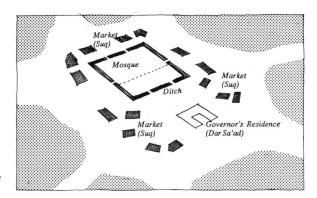

Stage 1: *Two separate and distant buildings*

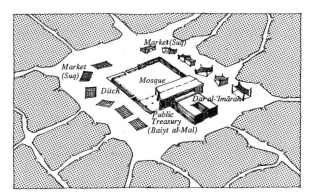

Stage 2: *Mosque moved to the side of Dar al-'Imārah*

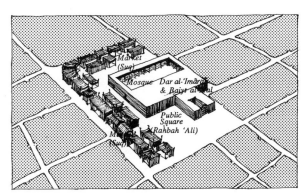

Stage 3: *One building and one square*

FIGURE 3.5 The Initial Core of Kufah and the Changing Relationship Between the Mosque, the Dar al-Imarah, and the Market.

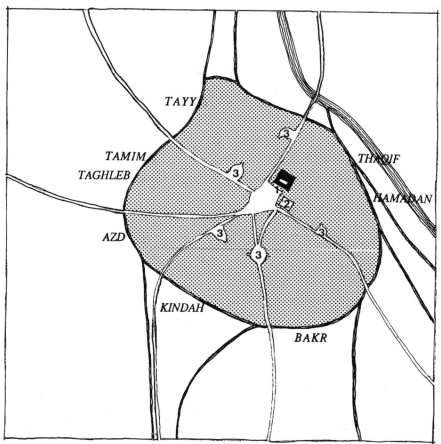

1. Mosque 2. Qasr 3. Maiydan with prayer place

FIGURE 3.6 A Schematic Organization of the Plan of Kufah (Massignon's reconstruction).

tions assigned to them, and these appropriately appear on al-Janabi's plan. Al-Tabari further relates that, at times, two or three small tribes shared the site between the two roads. This could refer to the fact that a standard *khutah* was simply divided between them or what Tabari may have meant by his use of the term *Ikhlat*, or "mixing up."[63] Of course the issue involved here is whether the streets, as they were laid out, determined the general form of the *khutat* or instead were determined by them.

In a recent dissertation on territoriality and responsibility in the Muslim environment, Akbar argues that *Ikhlat* does not mean that the tribes shared the same *khutah*, and instead he concludes that the *khutat* had various sizes.[64] To support his claim, Akbar cites al-Baladhri's report that the *Khutah* to the west of the *Sahah* accommodated 12,000 inhabitants, while the one to its east accommodated only 8,000.[65] Based on that, Akbar concludes that the areas between the roads were not equal.[66] One can easily differ with Akbar on this issue simply because *khutat* of equal sizes or occupying equal areas may have accommodated different populations and possessed different densities. In fact,

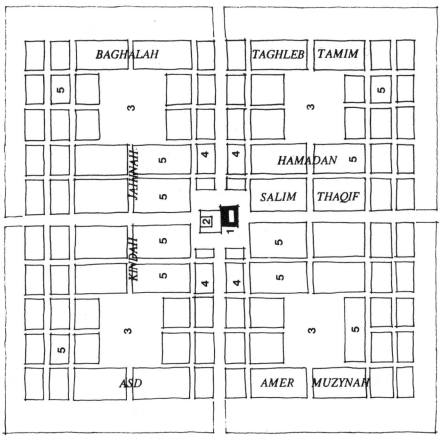

1. *Mosque* 2. *Dar al-Imarah* 3. *Square (Maiydan)* 4. *Quarters for Amir's Companions*
5. *Residential quarters*

FIGURE 3.7 The Plan of Kufah, 638 A.D. (Al-Janabi's reconstruction).

if we refer to al-Tabari, we get the impression that the city was divided into *khutat* that were assigned to different average-sized tribes.[67] From this, I believe that it is more likely that the *khutah*, at least in the beginning, was neither a social unit nor a standard neighborhood. It simply was a planning unit serving the purposes of land subdivision among military tribal groups.

Within each *khutah*, al-Ya'aqubi reports that each tribe subdivided its own place and that most tribes allocated their own mosque, cemetery, and burial place at the center of its own *khutah* within a square that was referred to as *rahbah*.[68] Al-Tabari describes the residential quarters or *mahals* as encampments placed "between" the roads. According to him, when the number of people in any tribe was larger than the average, the tribe was assigned more than one *khutah*. With the increase in population due to immigration, the tribal *khutah* seems to have also accommodated the *rawadef*, or newcomers. When a new group of immigrants arrived, the tribes made room for them within their own *khutah*.[69] This could have been achieved in one of two ways: families could have admitted relatives into their own dwellings, or newcomers could have been assigned unbuilt space within the *khutah*. Either case supports the view that even though the *khutat* may have been of similar geometrical sizes and configuration, they must have accommodated a variety of densities.

To gain a better understanding of this process, one may benefit from comparing it with a similar contemporary processes. In many developing countries today, the influx of rural people into the peripheries of existing urban areas has brought about a similar settlement process: squatting. Most observers of this process agree that the new immigrant rural families are first admitted into the dwellings of their relatives or the dwellings of families from their original villages. As a second step, once they are more settled in terms of the job market, they move onto a nearby vacant site and build their own illegal dwelling space from makeshift materials.[70]

It is very likely that the settlement process in Kufah was not dramatically different from this contemporary squatting process, despite the difference in time and place. One possible difference, however, was that in Kufah the system was more organized because the *khutat* represented a planned integration of the

---

1. Mosque 2. Dar al-Imarah 3. Sahah (Main Square) 4. Suq (Market) 5. Tribal Rahbas (Prayer place & burial grounds) 6. Individual Khutah (Mahal) 7. Manahej (Main Street)

FIGURE 3.8 (FACING PAGE) A Schematic Reconstruction of the General Organization and Urban Elements of Kufah.

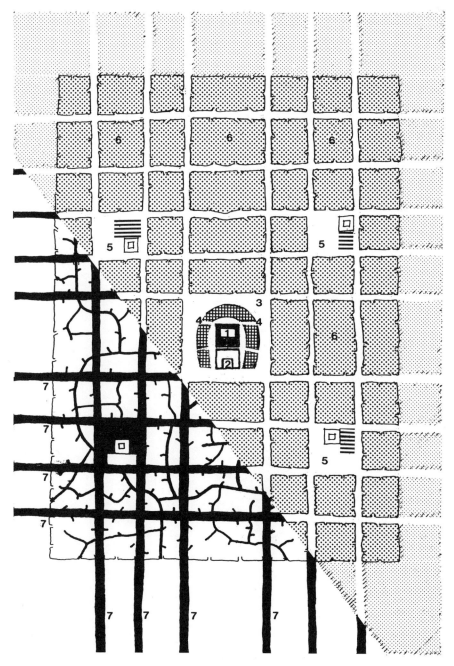

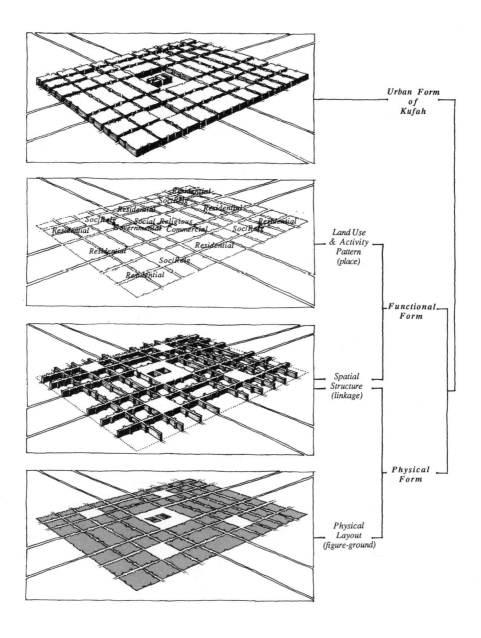

FIGURE 3.9 Kufah's Urban Form Analyzed.

late newcomers by including unbuilt spaces that could accommodate them.

It is reasonable to conclude that the *khutat* of Kufah was mainly a schematic plan marked out on the land, designating a geometrical planning grid (FIGURES 3.8 and 3.9). The general organization and its resulting block structure (FIGURE 3.10) were not physically defined and did not necessarily correspond to the social unit that occupied it — the tribe. It is possible that, on implementation, the plan became more irregular and that the grid form remained only an idea described in the different chronicles. Like Basrah, the overall form of early Kufah was thus the outcome of two separate and, at times, conflicting interests: the authority of the state and the will of the inhabitants. Unlike Basrah, the settlement process in Kufah was more organized and the general layout was at least planned on-site.

The division of responsibility in the early days seems to have prevented any further conflicts between the people and the state. The army general or governor, representing the authority of the state, took charge of establishing a general structure. The individual represented by his tribe was in charge of giving form to his immediate environment. It was this relationship between the individual and the state that shaped the physical form of the early Muslim city. Compromises on both sides were ultimately responsible for giving a place its characteristic morphology. Further explorations of the dynamics of urban administration are necessary if we seek a comprehensive understanding of the forces that shaped the early Muslim city.

THE ADMINISTRATION OF GARRISON TOWNS

In most instances the physical form of a town is a function of its urban function and administrative structure. This is probably true in the case of Muslim garrison towns, especially with regard to the role of the governors or administrators whose decisions shaped such towns.

Continuing a tradition that started during the prophets' time, the first Caliph Abu Bakr appointed governors, or *Walis*, for regions not yet conquered. Wherever he assembled an army and selected a commander to lead it, it was automatically assumed that the commander-in-chief would become the governor of the to-be-conquered city or region.[71] The governors of different cities seemed to have carried different titles, even though they may have been assigned the same tasks. This was true in the case of Basrah and Kufah. Most chronicles refer to the governor of Basrah as '*Amel al-Basrah*, while the governor of Kufah, who enjoyed the same status, seemed to have carried the title of *Amir al-Kufah*.[72]

Regardless of his title, a governor's responsibility included administering the affairs of the garrison, maintaining law and order through the implementation of *shari'ah*, collecting taxes, financially managing the treasury, maintaining the religion by leading the public prayers as *Imam*, delivering the *khutbah*, or sermon, and organizing the *hajj*, or the pilgrimage to Mecca.[73] The combination of all such responsibilities under early Muslim governors of garrison towns was probably an extension of the authority exercised by Prophet Muhamad in Madinah.

Because the socioeconomic relationships and the forms of ownership and production that the Arabs found in the conquered lands were as yet unknown in Arabia, the Arabs did not at first manipulate the existing complex apparatus of urban administration. During the period of the early caliphs, the cities and the vast territories conquered by the Arabs remained a collection of regions with different systems of urban administration.[74] The Arabs also left untouched both the socioeconomic regime and the administrative fiscal apparatus in the lands

FIGURE 3.10 (ABOVE AND FACING PAGE) Two Views Representing a Possible Reconstruction of Kufah as Planned.

they conquered, and at times even copied this apparatus in their new garrison towns.[75] These actions led Belyaev to the radical conclusion that the Arabs failed to show any interest in the land as a means of production because they simply considered all the land that fell under their domain as the property of the *aumah* (also *umma*) or the entire Muslim community. Belyaev further contends that the conquerors, busied with their loot, became merely an upper dominant structure superimposed on the local feudal society to exploit the subject population.[76]

Of course, Jahez's story, discussed earlier, regarding the rush to possess land in the garrison regions, whether arable for farming or urban for building, discredits Belyaev's contention. Salem's view on the issue of the Arabs' administration of the early towns seems more reasonable. According to Salem, the Arabs adopted all the early administrative systems that did not contradict their political hierarchy or religious beliefs. Whatever could not be accommodated by these, they simply changed.[77]

It makes perfect sense that a new rising power would utilize already existing and working systems in lands belonging to people who spoke different languages and possessed different cultures. There are many examples of urban systems adopted by the Arabs. In Persia, they continued the administrative Sassanian *diwan* system and implemented a similar system for the garrison towns in Iraq. In Syria and Egypt they adopted the Byzantine urban hierarchy of *qurah* and *rustaq*.[78]

Garrison towns were not independent entities but were part of a larger urban hierarchy. Many decisions that ultimately shaped the physical form of those towns were rendered by the caliph in Madinah. The governor of the town, being the representative of the caliph, held the authority of action. In the early years the office of the governor combined the two main functions of local government: judicial and executive. It was not until Caliph 'Umar introduced the position of the *qadi*, or judge, to be in charge of implementing *shari'ah* laws that a separation between such functions occurred.[79]

The relationship between the caliphs and their governors is of some importance in our attempt to understand the forces that shaped the Muslim city. From the cases we have looked at, we have seen that the governor was, in fact, a mediator between the caliph and the local population. Based on his political and religious authority the caliph had the power and the responsibility, at least in the early days of Islam, to legislate for the entire *aumah* or community of the faithful. But the local inhabitants of the garrison towns, as we have seen, had other needs and aspirations that at the time conflicted with caliphal vision. It was the responsibility of the governor to use all his political expertise to mediate a compromise between the authority of the Muslim state and the will of the individual Muslim. Many governors succeeded in playing that role, and some, as in the case of Sa'ad, went the further step of introducing physical planning solutions that deviated from the rule of the caliph, but still respected, at least in spirit, the authority of the state.

FROM 'UMAR TO 'UTHMAN: THE CALIPHATE AND THE MUSLIM GARRISON TOWN

Since the beginning of Islam, *jehad*, or the religious duty of holy war, set the Islamic community against the world. The war machine established by Abu Bakr, the first caliph, generated an inner momentum that could not be stopped. The wave of conquest beyond Arabia set in motion under Abu Bakr was accelerated by 'Umar, climaxed under him, and terminated under his successor 'Uthman.[80] But it is 'Umar who should be credited with the pattern of Arab settlement and the general planning of the early Muslim garrison towns, and it was clear from the beginning that 'Umar was intent on preventing the Arab nation from becoming an urban one.

'Umar was against the Arabs' settling down, especially in existing, newly conquered cities with a non-Muslim population. When settlement was inevitable, he was determined to maintain the roughness of the Arab fighters by inhibiting them from building permanent structures or utilizing more-durable material. Finally, when 'Umar was forced, at the end of his caliphate, to accept the reality of Arab Muslim urbanization and the new form of Islamic urban existence, the Muslim city, he attempted to ensure the purity and simplicity of the city by regulating the building and settlement process and by imposing restrictions on the type and extent of inhabitants' building activities.

The Islamic empire and its ensuing urbanization were to a great extent by-products of 'Umar's mentality and vision. 'Umar's actions and opinions indicate that he felt a strong, anti-urban sentiment. The resulting pattern of urbanization and its manifestations in physical form seem to have occurred in spite of his actions and not because of them. One can even argue that 'Umar was the master planner of the Muslim garrison town because his decisions determined the form of its early core. During 'Umar's reign, the form of garrison towns embodied the puritanical ideals of Islam. Indeed, the character of 'Umar, who was idealized by the Muslims for his modesty, sagacity, indifference to comfort, high sense of duty, and selfless interest in the service of Islam, is to be credited with much of the form of the early *amsar*.

But the ideals of 'Umar were not the only ones which had influence. 'Umar was assassinated in 23/644. His successor, 'Uthman, took a different view toward the administration of conquered territories. 'Uthman was the third of the orthodox caliphs. Belonging to the Quraishi aristocracy of Mecca, he was accustomed to a lavish lifestyle. One of his major actions directly preceding his succession to the caliphate was the construction of a house for himself in Madinah. Several chronicles report that the house, unlike all others in the city, was seven stories high and was constructed of stone with metal doors.[81] 'Uthman, a rich man, enjoyed good attire, good food, and good entertainment within the confines of Islam. During his reign his companions built more-elaborate structures instead of the simple houses they were used to.[82]

As he ascended to the caliphate, 'Uthman appointed new governors for the *amsar*. In doing so, he favored several members of his clan. 'Uthman's life and attitude seems to have served as the model for his appointees. Many historians report that, during the first years of 'Uthman's caliphate, the *amsar* witnessed a relaxation of the strict controls put in place by 'Umar.[83] Under 'Uthman, Basrah and Kufah gained enough momentum as settlements to demand a degree of independence that the caliph did not necessarily want to give out. Being a relatively weak caliph, 'Uthman was not successful in enforcing his view. In fact, 'Amr and Mu'awiyah, the respective governors of Egypt and Syria, came near to overt disobedience.[84]

The difference between the personalities and actions of 'Umar and 'Uthman may shed some light on the process of transformation of garrison towns, especially as this applies to the symbolic role of buildings in Muslim cities.

With regard to 'Umar, no story is more significant in understanding his actual intentions than the events surrounding the building of Dar Sa'ad in Kufah. As mentioned earlier, Sa'ad, who was 'Umar's governor in Kufah, had built for himself a residence in the center of the town using bricks and stones pulled away from the remains of a nearby Sasanian temple or palace.[85] As the city grew and became more populated, Sa'ad decided to shut permanently the entrance to the residence facing the market because of the noise produced by people there. Since it was one of the few major buildings in the city, Kufans started to refer to the residence as the Palace of Sa'ad.

The chronicles report that when the story of the residence reached Caliph

'Umar in Madinah, he was very dismayed at what appeared to him selfish actions by one of his commanders. The chronicles further relate that 'Umar sent a message to Sa'ad with Muhamad ibn Muslemah, who was also assigned the duty of burning down the door of Sa'ad's palace. Ibn Muslemah performed his duty and delivered to Sa'ad a letter from 'Umar stating:

> *It has come to my attention that you have built yourself a castle which people call the palace of Sa'ad; and that you have made between yourself and your people a door; so be advised that it is no more your palace but the palace of your dreams; so leave it for a more modest house and do not make the gate a barrier that would prevent the people from coming to you for their rights.*[86]

Since this story was reported by two prominent Muslim historians, there is no reason to suspect its accuracy, especially since it fits very well with 'Umar's overall profile. And knowing of 'Uthman's attitudes toward building, it is doubtful that he would have looked upon Sa'ad's actions so negatively or reprimanded him as 'Umar did.

Another important story, showing the differences between 'Umar and 'Uthman and how these affected the form of Muslim garrison towns, is what al-Tabari relates as 'Umar's attitudes toward Arab immigration to the new territories. 'Umar seems to have been concerned that the Arabs' strong desire to immigrate to the conquered territories would rapidly depopulate mainland Arabia. To prevent this from happening, 'Umar established and enforced strict immigration controls. When 'Uthman took over the caliphate, he abandoned 'Umar's controls. Large numbers of Arabs left Arabia during 'Uthman's reign and settled the new *amsar*.[87]

A third incident indicating the difference between 'Umar and 'Uthman is the story related by both al-Tabari and al-Baladhri regarding the financial administration of Fustat, another garrison town in Egypt. As the towns were developing into more complex entities, the need arose to appoint fiscal agents to administer or assist in the administration of the financial affairs. But when 'Uthman's fiscal agent arrived in Fustat, its governor, Amr, sent him back with a letter of objection that stated: "You can not appoint one man to hold the cow's horn and another to milk it."[88] Compare this incident, which shows the relationship between 'Uthman and his governor 'Amr, to the other earlier incident between 'Umar and his governor, Sa'ad, regarding the building of the palace, and the situation becomes very clear.

'Uthman was definitely a weaker caliph if compared to 'Umar, and when he tried to seize power he was nearly always met with resistance by the residents of the *amsar*. Under 'Uthman the governors of the garrison towns acquired more independence and took charge of the affairs of their own cities instead of waiting for orders or advice from Madinah. Simply put, 'Uthman's caliphate represented another stage in the development of Muslim garrison towns.

THE FORM OF THE MUSLIM GARRISON TOWN

It is reasonable to conclude that until the death of 'Umar in 23/644, garrison towns were planned, run, and administered according to some Islamic ideals of modesty and simplicity. The physical form of such towns was primarily a product of negotiations. While the general organization may have been set by the state, the internal organization was negotiated between the initial inhabitants and the governor in charge. The overall form of a garrison town was also a result of negotiations between the caliph, who was upholding the *aumah*, the Islamic ideal of the community of faithful, and his assigned governor, who was more in tune to the actual problems and needs of the inhabitants.

'Umar tried to establish in Basrah and Kufah the ideal Islamic settlement. By insisting on maintaining some heterogeneity in the population of the new garrison towns, 'Umar was attempting to diffuse the nomadic tribalism of the early Muslim Arabs.[89] Under 'Umar, garrison towns may have been in part a product of the state's program to break the powers of the independent nomadic groups which participated in the conquest for their own economic gain.

During later years, the garrison towns of Iraq became the centers of early Islamic culture. In them the militant Arabs had the chance to assimilate and refine their practices, theology was developed as a system of interpreting Islamic modes of behavior, and Arabic grammar as a symbol of Arabism was written down and codified. This formalized the Arabic language and institutionalized its use as the official tongue for all Muslims for years to come.[90]

Basrah and Kufah were the first prototypes of planned Muslim cities. They possessed similar features and to some extent conformed to the stereotypical image of a Muslim city. Setting aside the symbolic acts of 'Umar, it is obvious that the form of the two cities was a product of commonsense planning that represented Arab *bedwin* or nomadic tribal mentality. This does not deny Basrah and Kufah, in their early day, their Islamic identity. But there is no telling of what forms the Arabs would have created had they been given total freedom in the construction of the garrison towns. It is possible that the Arabs would have built structures more representative of Arab colonial intentions and less representative of Islam had they not had a very determined and religiously dedicated man like 'Umar as their caliph during that crucial period of urban genesis. Basrah and Kufah, and possibly other garrison towns, were planned as egalitarian Muslim communities and not as expressions of colonial power.

The reconstruction of Muslim garrison towns and the relationships of their typical elements may help us understand the origins of Arab Muslim planning concepts and assist us in decoding its symbolism. From the little we know, it appears that the mosque was not initially meant to be a permanent structure. Also the *Dar al-Imarah*, or the governor's residence, was not intended as a seat for government. In fact, references to it as an administrative unit disappear by the end of the eighth century. The *khutat*, or residential quarters, though located along ethnic and tribal lines, were geometric, but not necessarily orthogonal, planning units that served the purpose of land subdivision. Although their inhabitants showed common social features, the *khutat* were mainly residential neighborhoods and not the tightly bound social units portrayed in the stereotype. Since they were mainly established as army bases, Muslim garrison towns had no walls, gates, or citadels.

The relationship of these elements to each other is also of importance in understanding Arab Muslim planning intentions. The *Dar al-Imarah* and the mosque were not intended as one unit or structure. Joining them together was a matter of convenience and necessity. A *suq*, or a market, usually sprung outside of the mosque. Although the close association of the *suq* and the mosque was condoned by the caliph, when the relationship interfered with the religious and political functions of the settlement or the will of the governor, the market was relocated. Both Basrah and Kufah show different physical solutions accommodating the functions of the market, but in both cases, and contrary to the stereotype, several decentralized markets existed. In fact, the market outside of the city fabric seems to have played a more important economic role in the life of those towns than the market in front of the mosque.

A typical Muslim garrison town also had a major square at its center. This space, which was called the *sahn*, *sahah*, or *rahbah*, served the needs of the state and was its sole property.[91] It made a lot of sense to allocate the public buildings and functions in or around that square. Its centrality, as well as the centrality of the adjoining public buildings within the settlement, was probably a by-product of the process of laying out the town that followed an order that dictated

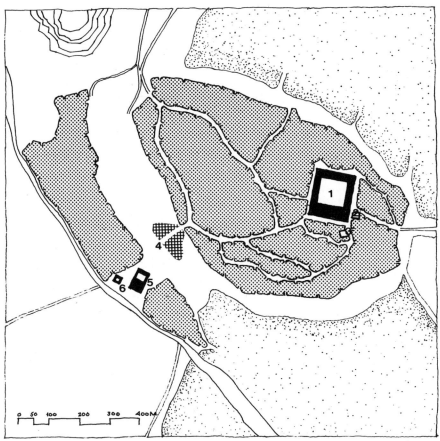

1. Prophet's Mosque 2. 'Uthman's house 3. 'Umar's house 4. Market 5. Musalla 6. 'Umar's Mosque

FIGURE 3.11 The Plan of Madinah After Mustafa.

the allocation of the public domain first.

In analyzing the form of the garrison towns, it is interesting to note that much of this model used to describe them bears striking similarity to Madinah, the capital of the Muslims under 'Umar (**FIGURE 3.11**). Since most of the commanders of the Arab armies and the governors of the garrison towns came from Madinah, it seems clear that they were at least attempting to replicate what they had back home.[92]

Another way of looking at the issue may arise from analyzing the resemblance to be found between the form of the garrison town and the general arrangement of the troops in a Muslim army encampment described by later writers[93] (FIGURE 3.12). It is important to note that army camps did not develop this order until Ottoman times. However, the similarity between the two layouts is significant, although it does not conform with proper chronological

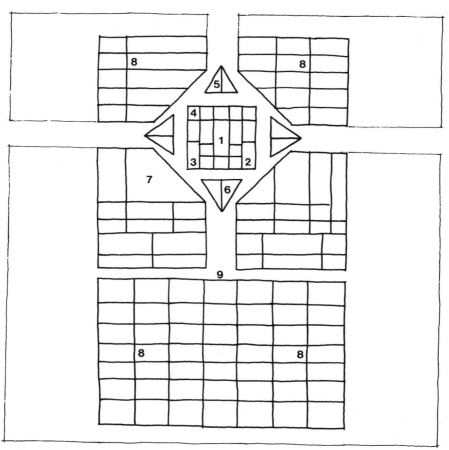

1. King/Caliph 2. Prayer place 3. Treasury 4. Kitchen 5. Royal Guards 6. Police 7. Administrators 8. Garrison 9. Ditch

FIGURE 3.12 The General Arrangement of a Muslim Army Encampment. (Zaydan's reconstruction)

sequence. In such an encampment, the commander occupied the center and was surrounded by his close advisers. A small space separated him from the rest of the troops, and close to that space was the area allocated for prayer. Different tribal troops, lumped together to form blocks of fighting men, constituted the rest of the encampment. Other service functions, like food or medicine, were peripheral. So it is possible that earlier Muslim troop encampments served as prototypes for the Muslim garrison town.

But this was the initial basis, and with the death of Caliph 'Umar in 23/644, a new era started for Muslim garrison towns. During 'Uthman's reign, the governors gained more control of their towns and stopped consulting with the caliph on matters of urban form.[94] This could have occurred because the territories had expanded to an extent that made it difficult for the caliph to centrally administer them from Madinah, because of the increasing role of the *amsar* and the increasing power held by the aristocracy in charge of administering them, and because most of the essential planning issues had already been decided upon. Whatever the causes, individual governors' hold over the *amsar* became so strong that some governors, such as Muawiyah of Damascus, started to assume the unofficial role of monarch and the official title of *Amir* or "prince."[95]

During the ensuing period the form of a garrison town was determined more by the individual will and acts of its governor than by Islamic religious principles or administrative rationale. This change put an end to the earlier Islamic and somewhat democratic process set in place by 'Umar. It was, however, this new attitude of independence from Madinah that allowed the garrison towns to be populated, enabled the immigrants to build, and permitted the development of an Islamic architecture and built form.

It is ironic that during the reign of a strong and influential caliph like 'Umar, whose decisions changed the face of the Middle East, garrison towns were not permitted to grow and acquire their equivalent architectural forms. It is even more ironic that it was during the reign of 'Uthman, the weakest of all orthodox caliphs, that garrison towns achieved a definition for their architecture and urban form that was more representative of their true urban reality. This established them as an an important category in the history of Muslim cities.

IV

URBAN TRANSFORMATIONS IN EARLY ISLAM
ARABIZATION OR ISLAMIZATION OF EXISTING CITIES

> *It was time to symbolize the majesty of the new religion,*
> *embodied in the majesty of the new state in structures*
> *comparable to. . . those of Europe.*[1]
>
> PHILIP HITTI

The Arab takeover of the central Middle East was an extremely important victory for the new religion. The lands of Islam had come to include several mature cities belonging to earlier, well-established civilizations. The Muslim Arabs' reaction to the art, architecture, and urban forms of this newly conquered Christian world was a very mixed one: initial awe and admiration was followed by a feeling of disregard, rejection, and contempt. Finally, the attitudes of the Arabs toward the architecture of the conquered people changed to acceptance, understanding, and later to competition.

The anecdote related to us through a Christian source from this era, as discovered by Oleg Grabar, can best explain this Arab attitude.[2] The story has it that a treaty had been signed between Christians and Muslims in a town that was to change hands. One day before the actual exchange took place, a Muslim rider practicing horsemanship accidentally damaged the eye of Emperor Heraclius's statue in the Christian part of the town. When the Christians protested this accident, the local Muslim governor agreed to repair the damage. This, however, was not enough for the Christians, who insisted that the statue of the Muslim caliph be similarly defaced, and this the Muslim governor seems to have agreed to.

Although the Ummayads encouraged sculptures, it is unlikely that a statue glorifying a caliph was ever sculpted during those early years because of Islam's rejection of figurative sculptures. But if it was, one may think that the Muslim governor must have been aware of its symbolic significance. Yet he agreed to have the eyes of the caliph's statue put out because he simply did not believe as deeply as his Christian counterparts in the significance of an image. Perhaps this story portrays the attitude of the early Muslim Arabs as a people who did not care so much for the iconographic symbolism of their artifacts.

Using the original Arab chronicles, I will try in this chapter to examine the following questions: What were the early attitudes of the Arabs toward building, especially in existing cities? Why did their initial indifference change to active involvement? What brought about this transformation, and what were the circumstances that surrounded it? Throughout I will try to stick to my initial agenda of looking at snapshots of the takeover process. I will not offer a comprehensive history of any city nor will I be exhaustive in surveying the contemporary literature. My main intent is to analyze whether or not the transformation that occurred in Arab Muslim attitudes was representative of a maturing Islamic ideology or reflective of an Arab mentality and changing urban experience.

In a variety of works, Oleg Grabar has answered many of the questions posed above, especially as they relate to the artifacts of early Islamic civilization. Concentrating on the major urban elements that form the core of a typical Muslim city and their relationship to each other, I will attempt to offer answers to some of those questions.

THE ARABS IN SYRIA AND THE TAKEOVER OF DAMASCUS

In their attempt to consolidate the new Islamic state, the Arabs adopted the policy of building new towns, especially in places such as Iraq, as a means of redistributing the Arab population. Why did the Arabs not pursue a similar policy in Syria? There is no one answer to this question, but it is possible that Syrian cities, which were much smaller in size in comparison to their Middle Eastern counterparts, were not perceived as centers of entertainment that could spoil the Arabs' fighting spirit.

This may also have been the case because most of the Syrian towns were taken over peacefully as a result of treaties rather than by wars. The Arabs may not have felt the need to isolate themselves from the local people with whom they did not engage in battle. In addition, the Arab conquest of Syria threatened to disrupt its traditional prosperity. To prevent this from happening, the organizers of the conquest and the early governors (most of whom were from the Ummayad clan) took measures to prevent further Arab resettlement in Syrian cities so as to preserve the prosperity for their own tribe.[3] This may also have contributed to the maintenance of the existing pre-Arab urban structure.

In any case, the story of what the Arabs did with the Syrian cities is of importance because it adds another chapter to the history of Muslim urbanism, that of the Arabs as colonizers. The transformation that Syrian cities underwent reveals much about Arab mentality and identity. An analysis of the behavior of Arabs in Syrian cities leads to an understanding of the symbolism embedded in the adaptive reuse of urban form. This symbolism is different from that of a new city, which more likely represents the true urban intentions of the Arabs. If Basrah and Kufah were good examples of the latter, then Damascus, the most important of all Syrian cities, may serve as an excellent example of the former.

There are as many versions of the story of the fall of Damascus as there are Arab chroniclers.[4] Most accounts, however, agree that Arab forces first occupied the *ghutah* (the lush green area that surrounded Damascus and provided it with fresh produce).

The Arab forces surrounding the city were divided into two groups, one camping on the eastern side, and the other stationed in front of the western gate. There is a disagreement on who was in command. For example, al-Baladhri identifies Khaled ibn al-Walid as the commander of the eastern garrison and Abu 'Ubaidah as the commander of the western one. According to al-Baladhri's account, the Arabs surrounded Damascus for fourteen days after which Abu 'Ubaidah's forces engaged in a skirmish with the guards of the gate. It is then said that the bishop of Damascus, fearing the possible destruction of his churches, rushed to the other commander, Khaled, and agreed to let him enter the city peacefully on the condition that he sign a treaty promising that the Arabs would not take over the churches and houses of the Christians and that Christian lives would be spared if they paid the usual Jeziah tax required of all non-Muslims.[5]

Al-Tabari concurs with most of al-Baladhri's story and adds that the forces of Abu 'Ubaidah and Khaled entered the city from two different gates, marched into Damascus, and met at an area of the bazaar named by al-Tabari as *al-Nahasin*, or "the coppersmiths," and by al-Baladhri as *al-Zaiatin*, or "the oil merchants."[6]

Writing a few centuries later, Ibn 'Asaker (571/1175) adds more details to the stories of al-Baladhri and al-Tabari. According to Ibn 'Asaker, Khaled was the commander who entered the city forcefully from the eastern gate after engaging in a short battle, while Abu 'Ubaidah seems to have entered peacefully from the opposite gate. Ibn 'Asaker uses the evolution of the mosque of Damascus as evidence to this sequence of events. He argues that only the eastern side of the church was taken over by the Muslims and transferred into a mosque while the western side was preserved to perform its same function.

Ibn 'Asaker believes that the Arabs would have taken over the church in its entirety had it not been for Abu 'Ubaidah's treaty with the Christians and his peaceful entry from the western Jabiah gate. Although Ibn 'Asaker does not clearly state that, he implies that the western side of the church was only spared because the Muslims who entered the city from the west under Abu 'Ubaidah had to conform with an agreement that dictated respect for the Christian places of worship and prevented them from looting Christian property in this part of town.[7]

Caetain's work, which challenged Abu 'Ubaidah's early presence or participation in the Damascus campaign, cast some doubt on the validity of these stories.[8] But Elisseeff, writing on Damascus for the *Encyclopedia of Islam*, proposed a resolution of this contradiction by introducing to the picture what he calls the "second conquest of Damascus."[9] Elisseeff reminds us that in the spring of 15/636, an army commanded by Theodorus, brother of Heraclius, made its way to Damascus. Khaled, who was then amir of Damascus, evacuated the city and situated himself in Yarmuk in preparation for the Byzantine army. After successfully defeating the Byzantine forces, Khaled was removed from his post by the then new Caliph 'Umar and was ordered to return to Madinah. He was then replaced by Abu 'Ubaidah, who in capturing the city for the second time made his reputation as its conqueror[10] (FIGURE 4.1).

Setting aside Caetani's argument, Sabanu engages in a comparative examination of the chronicles' treatment of the history of Damascus.[11] According to this reconstruction, when Khaled stormed the city from its eastern gate the Christians rushed to Abu 'Ubaidah and signed a treaty with him and let him into the city through the Jabiah gate. Abu 'Ubaidah, who had promised the Christians the safety of their lives and structures, entered the city peacefully, only to meet the other conquering group led by Khaled, which by now was making claim to the city. While Khaled's forces were looting Damascus the two commanders argued. Khaled insisted that the Christian residents did not have any rights because they resisted his forces, but Abu 'Ubaidah, who had signed the treaty, argued otherwise. They finally agreed on enforcing Abu 'Ubaidah's treaty, at least until they consulted with the caliph. 'Umar, who had just taken

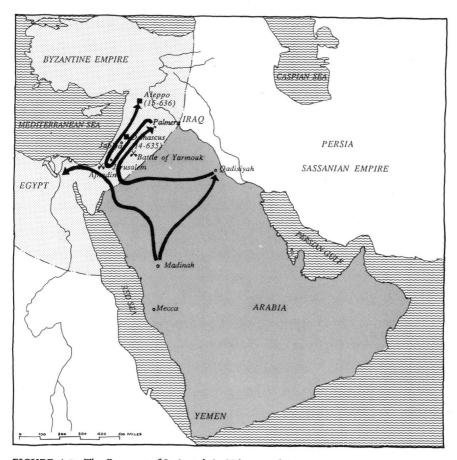

FIGURE 4.1 The Conquest of Syria and the Takeover of Damascus.

over as caliph, supported Abu 'Ubaidah's position and did not waste any time
before deposing Khaled from his role as commander.[12]

Knowing of all of these different versions of the conquest of Damascus, it
seems logical to believe that the two forces that took over the city disagreed on
the nature of this takeover and to assume that this disagreement may have had
some effect on the ensuing transformation of the city's urban form.

The fall of Damascus was an event of incalculable importance. The conquest
put an end to almost 1,000 years of Western supremacy. According to Elisseeff,
the people of Damascus received the conquerors with unreserved pleasure for

they felt nearer to them by race and language.[13] Although that may be partially true, it is still difficult to know the actual feelings of the people of Damascus toward their conquerors. Several chronicles mention that many residents left or fled Damascus at the time of the conquest.[14] This, of course, does not support Elisseeff's contention that the conquerors were received with open arms, but, as some have argued, it may be that those that left were only the ones working for the Byzantine administration.[15]

ARAB IMMIGRATION AND SETTLEMENT

Following the takeover of Damascus, Caliph 'Umar appointed Yazid ibn Sufiyan to govern the newly captured city. Damascus became a *Dar Hejrah*, and Arabs from all over the peninsula started to immigrate to it. In comparison to the situation in Iraq, much less is known about the pattern of Arab immigration and settlement in Syria, although here also the Arabs appear to have established several military encampments or garrison towns with specific administrative roles. Among these were the small towns of al-Jibayah and the al-Ramlah in the Golan and Palestine respectively. Unlike Basrah and Kufah in Iraq, however, the garrison towns of Syria never developed into important cities.

Donner suggested that one of the main reasons behind the relatively low-key status of the Syrian garrison towns could be attributed to the Arab's preference for settling in existing towns such as Damascus, Aleppo, and Hims.[16] Settling in existing towns was also what the Arabs preferred to do in Persia, but there, as we have observed earlier, they were ordered to move out and instructed to settle in new towns in an attempt by the Caliph 'Umar to separate them from the local population and to maintain their roughness as fighting soldiers. It is difficult to know why the Arabs in Syria were not asked to undergo a similar movement or if Caliph 'Umar even considered making such a demand of them.

Looking into the forces behind the limited Arab immigration to Syria and their settlement of rural land, Donner offers a few explanations. He suggests that the low level of migration to Syria was a reflection of the ruling elite's settlement policy. Syria, and particularly Damascus, was viewed by the Quraishys, who governed Damascus, as their own special preserve. Because of their long-standing commercial ties with Damascus before Islam, they were intent on keeping it to themselves, undisturbed by tribal feuds.[17] Perhaps Donner's interpretation is supported by the fact that most of the Quraishys preferred to fight on the Syrian front instead of the Iraqi one.[18]

DAMASCUS BEFORE THE ARABS

Throughout its history, Damascus had always been an important city. The first mention of it as a city dates to the eleventh century B.C. when it was a capital of a small Aramaic kingdom. Later, Damascus, with the whole of Syria, came successively under the rule of the Assyrians, the Babylonians, the Achaemenids, the Greeks, the Nabataeans, and finally the Romans.[19]

The conquest of Damascus by Alexander the Great in 333 B.C. was an important event for Damascus's urban form. Two general stages may be distinguished for this Hellenistic period: first, a Ptolemaic founding in the third century B.C., then the raising of the town to a capital in the first century B.C. by the Seleucids, which was immediately followed by the addition of a Greek colony to its side. During this time the Hellenistic urban planning system was introduced. The characteristic elements of this plan included the temple of Jupiter, the *agora*, the uniform grid, and the small blocks of houses on standard-size lots[20] (FIGURE 4.2).

Damascus came under the Romans in the first century B.C., and by the beginning of the second century A.D., under Hadrian, it was given the rank of metropolis. Before the end of the third century A.D. it was designated a colony. The Romans imposed a new urban plan that integrated the original Hellenistic town and the older Aramaic part into one entity.

The Roman plan was dominated by two great colonnaded streets. The first crossed the town from east to west like the *decumanus* of Roman cities, and on it lay several Roman arches. The second was the ancient road adjoining the temples and the *agora* which now was transformed into a forum. A *castrum* was also built in the northeast corner of the city. Under the Romans the city was given its rectangular shape, measuring 500 x 750 meters. It was surrounded by a defensive wall penetrated only by seven gates: the eastern gate, the Al-Jabiah gate to the west, three gates to the north including the Thomas Gate in its northeast, and two gates to the south[21] (FIGURES 4.3 and 4.4).

In 395 A.D. Damascus became part of the Byzantine Empire, and the church as a building type was introduced for the first time to the city. The temple of Jupiter which by now had fallen into disuse was rebuilt and transformed into a church dedicated to St. John the Baptist. Other buildings were also added in the *peribolus* or the space between the church walls and the outside walls of the temple. This included some arcades that later accommodated church supervised market activity. Several churches were also built during the Byzantine era.

These included the Church of the Cross, located on the northeastern side; the Church of the Maqslat, located midway along the *decumanus*; the Church of St. Mary close to the eastern gate of the city, and the Churches of St. Paul and the Jacobites inside the Thomas gate. For a variety of reasons, Byzantine churches did not survive the several centuries of Muslim rule. Many of them were dismantled and their wood and stone reused in the construction of Islamic buildings.[22]

The western hills of the city, later included in the Roman wall, also contained, in addition to the *castrum*, a Byzantine palace. The palace was used by some Byzantine governors, but both Ibn 'Asaker and Baladhri relate that the Byzantine governor's palace, at the Arab takeover, was located south of the Church of St. John, possibly on the *decumanus*.[23]

After the successive attempts on the City by the Ghassanids and the Sassanians, Damascus fell to the Arabs. By that time, the general weakening of governmental authority had brought about a disregard for building codes. Physical order in the city started to disintegrate, and although many encroachments on city streets had occurred, the grid was still functional and visible.[24]

FIGURE 4.2 (ABOVE AND FACING PAGE) Two Views Representing a Reconstruction of Damascus Before the Arab Conquest.

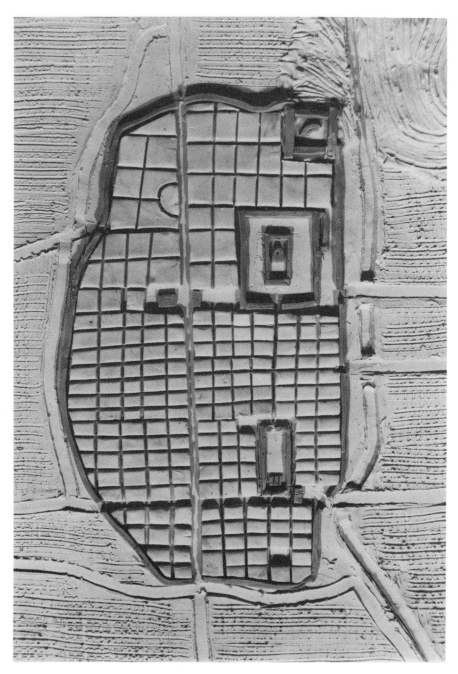

The Arabs seem to have been very impressed by the city's regularity, especially with its long *decumanus* which they called Al-Mustaqim, "the straight," a name that remained in use for almost ten centuries.

DAMASCUS UNDER THE ARABS: FUNCTIONAL AND FORMAL TRANSFORMATIONS

The domination of the conquerors did not at first bring any changes to the life of Damascus. As mentioned earlier, several groups of the Greek-speaking population fled the city, leaving behind a considerable amount of vacant property to be occupied by the incoming Arabs. This situation of vacant property was not unique to Damascus. Other Syrian cities such as Aleppo seem to have undergone a similar process.

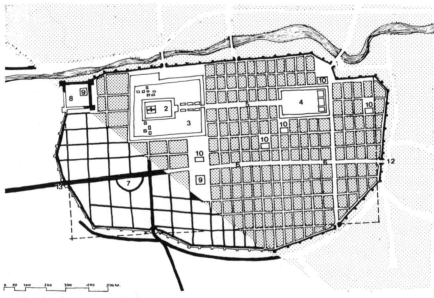

1. *Temple of Jupiter turned Church of St. John* 2. *Temenos* 3. *Peribolus with shops added* 4. *Agora turned Forum with shops* 5. *Colonnaded Street* 6. *Decumanus later named The Straight* 7. *Theater transformed to warehouses* 8. *Castrum* 9. *Byzantine Palace* 10. *Byzantine Church* 11. *Thomas Gate* 12. *Eastern Gate* 13. *Jabiah Gate*

FIGURE 4.3 The Plan of Byzantine Damascus at the Beginning of the Seventh Century Before the Arab Takeover, Based on Sauvaget, Elisseeff, and the Arab Chronicles.

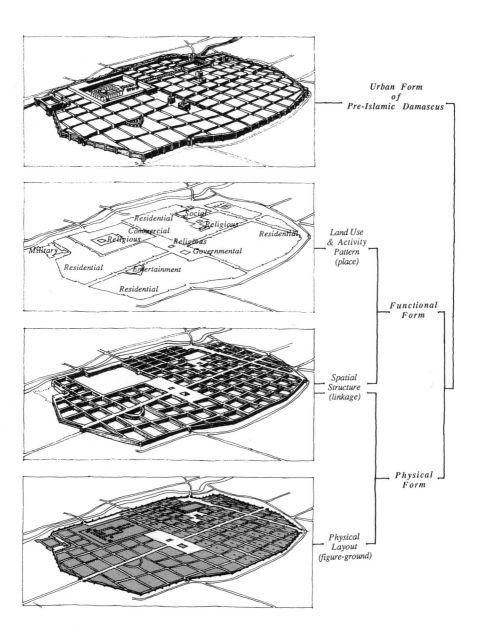

Urban Form
of
Pre-Islamic Damascus

Land Use
& Activity
Pattern
(place)

Functional
Form

Spatial
Structure
(linkage)

Physical
Form

Physical
Layout
(figure-ground)

Residential
Social
Commercial
Religious
Religious
Residential
Military
Religious
Governmental
Residential
Entertainment
Residential

FIGURE 4.4 The Urban Form of Pre-Islamic Damascus Analyzed.

> *Not all the vacant space in various Syrian towns was the result of headlong flight, however. There are many accounts that suggest that the Muslims made treaties with the inhabitants of some towns, among the terms of which was the stipulation that a certain amount of property within the city would be vacated by the citizens to make room for the Muslims.*[25]

Several chronicles, in fact, state that the Damascans were frequently asked to relinquish their houses for use by the Muslims as dwellings and mosques.[26]

There are, however, many stories in the various chronicles about the nature of the treaty the Arabs signed with the Christians. Al-Baladhri mentions, for example, that al-Waqidi, who allegedly saw the text of the treaty signed by Khaled (a debated issue in itself), reported that it did not contain any reference to the division of homes or churches. Many scholars looking into that issue have reached the conclusion that the details surrounding the takeover of Damascus belong to the systemization of subsequent generations of legal scholars seeking to rationalize the event.[27]

Whether it was due to voluntary evacuations or dispossession, the vacant houses of Damascus were gradually settled by the Muslim Arabs. As in the case of Kufah and Basrah, the Arabs started to be concerned with owning the land they lived on. During the settlement process many of them were granted *qatai'a* of agricultural land or urban dwellings.[28]

Although we know very little about where the Arabs lived exactly, we know that initially they did not live in any special quarters. The commanders of the different garrisons seem to have taken over a number of vacated houses in a variety of locations. We know, for example, of a Dar Khaled or a Dar Sa'ad. Both of these residences do not seem to have occupied any special location within the city.

Perhaps the most significant story in the Arab transformation of Damascus is that of its mosque. Again, there are a variety of accounts of what the Arabs did to create a place for worship for themselves in the city. The site that they ended up choosing was, of course, that of the former Church of St. John. Ibn Jubair contends that the Muslims, upon entering the city, divided the *kanisa*, or the "church," into two parts with the Muslims occupying the eastern half. This account is supported by the "fact" that Khaled entered the city by force from the eastern gate. The western half of the church remained in the hands of the Christians.[29]

This version is supported by a Christian account from the same period. According to Gallic Bishop Arculf, who visited Damascus in his travels around the year 50/670, there existed separate sanctuaries for each of the two communities. In this account, the mosque is described as being a *musalla*, situated against the eastern part of the southern wall of the *peribolus*.[30]

The alleged partitioning of the church was refuted by many scholars. Some, like De Geoje and Von Kremer, pointed out the impossibility of worship by the two different groups in so closely adjacent spaces. Others attributed this confusion to an error in translation. They claim that Ibn Jubair used the word *kanisa*, or "church," in its broad sense as the place for Christian prayer and was thus signifying the entire sanctuary, which included the church building and the space surrounding it, possibly enclosed by a wall.[31] Creswell finally resolved this confusion by reconciling different parts of those stories. He concluded that the church was never divided and that the Muslims simply took over the eastern half of the old temple or the *temenos* that was outside the church building.[32] During those early days the church remained intact (**FIGURE 4.5**).

Creswell's explanation seems to conform with what the Christians were guaranteed in their treaty with the Arabs, and it confirms the view that the

---

The Muslims and Christians entered by the same doorway, which was that of the original temple, placed on the south side where is now the great mihrab. Then the Christians turned to the west towards their church, and the Muslims to the right to reach their mosque.

FROM IBN SHAKIR

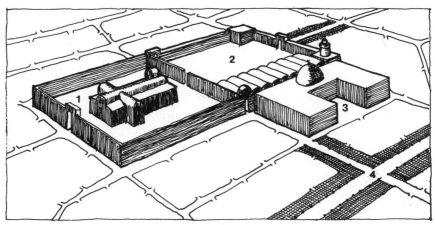

1. Church of St. John 2. Ummayad Mosque 3. Al-Khadra Palace 4. Market/Colonnade turned Bazaar

FIGURE 4.5 A Reconstruction of the Mosque of Damascus, the Church of St. John, and the Palace of Mu'awiyah, Based on Ibn 'Asaker.

Arabs simply took over the *parvis*, or the space outside the church, and used it as a prayer space. Many questions, however, remain unanswered. For example, how did the Muslim pray in that space? What were the physical and functional qualities of the space? Was any part of this space sheltered, and what may have been its relationship to the *qibla*?

As mentioned earlier, a few of the chronicles refer to the mosque that was adjacent to the church in Damascus as a *musala* or *musalla*. The word *musalla* is frequently used to denote a place or a space for prayers on special occasions.[33] A *musalla* did not have to be a building to perform its function. The word *musalla* was used first in Madinah to refer to the place outside the city where the Muslims gathered for the Eid prayer. It was only later, during the time of the Ummayad caliphs, that a structure was built in the *musalla* of Madinah and was appropriately named *Masjid al-Musalla*, or "The Mosque of Musalla."[34] Based on this precedent, it is possible to suggest that a similar process may have occurred in Damascus, a process in which the act of building was not in itself a perpetuator of the Arabization or Islamization of the city.

Although the story of the mosque is but one story in the history of the Damascus takeover, it is still of major significance in our attempt to understand the urban transformation of the city. The Arabs did not behave any differently with any of the other building types they occupied, and little or no structural changes seem to have occurred in Damascus, at least until the Ummayads made it their capital in 40/661.

DAMASCUS AS CAPITAL

The incidents that surrounded the deposition of Ali, the last of the orthodox caliphs, and his replacement with Mu'awiyah ibn Abi Sufian are very well known. Since he was already its governor, Mu'awiyah found it more convenient to bring the caliphate to Damascus.

> *Mu'awiyah's choice of Damascus as his capital was perhaps the most pregnant fact in its entire history. It started the city on its way to becoming for eighty-nine years mistress of the Muslim realm and key city in Medieval world affairs.*[35]

After Muhamad and 'Umar, Mu'awiyah stands out as one of the most competent men in the history of early Islam, and his name has become as inextricably associated with Damascus as Muhamad's has been with Mecca and

'Umar's with Madinah.

Building on his previous experiences as governor of the region, and following the already existing Byzantine model, Mu'awiyah founded the administrative institutions of Damascus; under him, Islam began to absorb more of the Mediterranean and less of the desert.[36] Mu'awiyah modified the caliphate and from the beginning appears to have had the intention of changing it into a monarchy. During his reign he gave himself the title of *malek*, or "king," claiming that he was no less important than the kings of the surrounding empires.[37] Although the term *malek* was detested by his Arab subjects and the practice of ruling as king was considered non-Islamic by the early Muslim jurists, Mu'awiyah went ahead with his plans to build a dynasty that could compete with the European ones around it.

As governor, Mu'awiyah seemed to have lived in one of the old Byzantine palaces in the city, but within a few years of having taken over as caliph he built himself a palace. Again, very little is known about the palace that Mu'awiyah took as his official residence. Several chronicles refer to it as Dar al-Khelafah, or the official residence of the caliph.[38] Why the term was introduced is somewhat of a mystery. In Madinah, the capital of the Muslims during the time of the orthodox caliphs, the residence of the caliph was usually referred to as Dar 'Umar, or Dar 'Uthman, following the name of the caliph himself. There the house of the caliph did not act as a seat of government because most of the orthodox caliphs perferred to hold their *majlis*, or court, in the mosque instead of their residences.[39]

It may be that the unsettled circumstances that surrounded Mu'awiyah's succession to the caliphate brought about his need to legitimize his position by building a palace that bore an official title. Mu'awiyah's palace was referred to as *al-Khadra'*, or the "green palace," because it supposedly possessed a large green dome. According to Ibn 'Asaker, the palace was built of bricks and placed adjacent to the south wall of the mosque which faced the *qibla*.[40] As this was the *qibla* side of the mosque, one is reminded here of a similar earlier precedent, that of the relationship of Dar al-Imarah to the mosque in both Basrah and Kufah.

It is doubtful that this relationship in Damascus was accidental, but it is difficult to trace it back to its earlier precedents or to establish that Mu'awiyah was trying to duplicate a pattern he had seen before. From Ibn 'Asaker, we know that the palace underwent several modifications during the reign of Mu'awiyah himself. He reports that, upon seeing the palace, the Byzantine ambassador to Damascus commented that "this is no palace for its top is for birds and its bottom is for fire." This seems to have prompted Mu'awiyah to enlarge the palace and rebuild it in stone.[41]

The palace of Mu'awiyah seems to have contained two distinct quarters: the first was his family residence and the second was the court, in which he conducted the administration of state affairs. In fact, the title "green palace" may have been given to the complex of administrative buildings of which Mu'awiyah's house was only a part, as was the case later in Abbasid Baghdad. According to Elisseeff, the green palace was not a new building but only a remodeling of the former Byzantine palace[42] (FIGURE 4.5). But even if Elisseeff is right, this should not reduce the importance of seeing the mosque and the caliph's quarters in early Damascus as one integral unit representing the unity of state and religion.

The Christians, whom the caliph depended upon, enjoyed a considerable degree of freedom of worship and practice in those early days. The religious barrier did not loom too high, and the caliph's tolerant policy brought many Christians into his court. For his tolerance, Mu'awiyah was repaid in undivided loyalty by his Christian subjects.[43]

Even though it was the capital under Mu'awiyah, the physical form and the

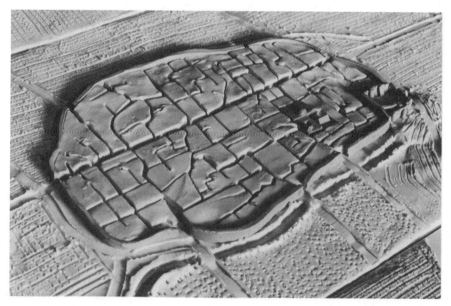

FIGURE 4.6 (ABOVE AND FACING PAGE) Two Views Representing a Reconstruction of Islamic Damascus.

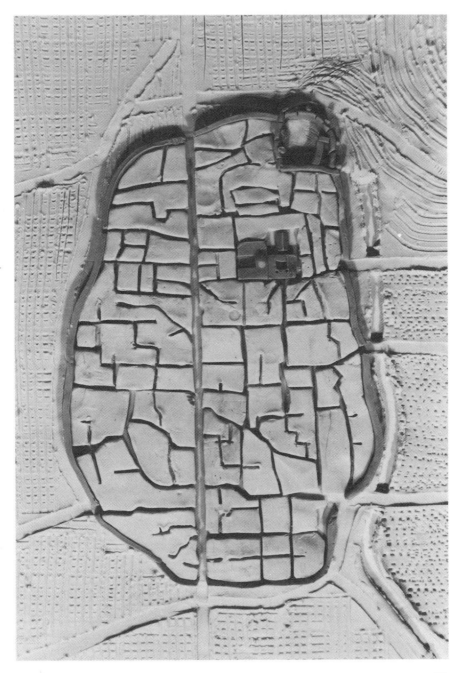

daily activities of Damascus did not change much. Greek was maintained as the language of administration, and the general image of the city remained the same in spite of the major cultural transformation it was undergoing and the accompanying changes in its physical form.[44] The alleged irrationality of the streets of Damascus and its spatial organization has been subject of a great debate (FIGURE 4.6). The prevailing idea among researchers is that the irregularity of the streets was a manifestation of some anarchic principles inherent in the Islamic urban system. This view has mainly been espoused by Jean Sauvaget, whose attempt to reconstruct the Greco-Roman plan of Damascus and Aleppo led him to the conclusion that the regularity of the streets was preserved down to the Islamic era but was lost under the influence of the Arabs[45] (FIGURES 4.7 and 4.8).

It was, however, De Planhol, as shown earlier, who popularized this idea and stigmatized all Islamic cities as cities lacking any order. De Planhol confused students of urbanism by suggesting that "the religion of Islam leads to a negation of urban order."[46] Von Grunebaum later pointed out that the decomposition of the Damascus grid had begun as early as the second century A.D., and

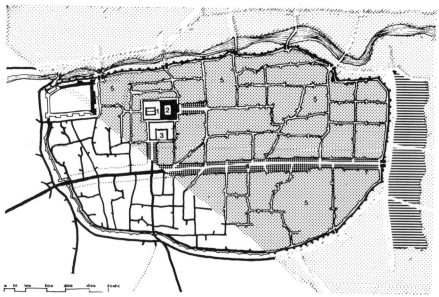

1. *Church of St. John* 2. *Ummayad Mosque* 3. *Al-Khadra Palace* 4. *Market/Colonnade*
5. *Residential Quarters* 6. *Cemeteries*

FIGURE 4.7 The Plan of Islamic Damascus, Based on Al-Munjid.

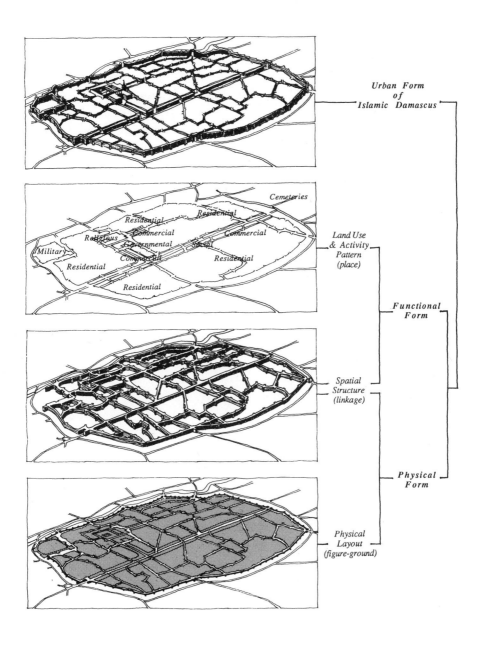

FIGURE 4.8 The Urban Form of Islamic Damascus Analyzed.

that the gradual forsaking of the geometric block structure was consummated under the Arabs.[47] Like Sauvaget, Von Grunebaum attributes the transformation to weakness of government authority.

Although this is partially true, it is difficult to know when this transformation was actually consummated and what were the forces that brought it about. We know, however, that the general image of the city was not radically changed by the Arab occupation and that whatever changes were taking place in its streets were part of an ongoing urban process (FIGURES 4.9 and 4.10).

The story of Damascus stands as proof that the early Arabs, especially in the case of existing cities, were not intent on creating a new urban image for the places they occupied. Unlike Basrah and Kufah, the Arabs in Damascus were intent on adopting much of what was already there and adapting themselves to their new environment. As caliph, Mu'awiyah's concern for the survival of his own regime and caliphal dynasty (FIGURE 4.11) superseded the Arabs' concern for establishing a new urban existence.

BUILDING DAMASCUS: CHANGES IN PHYSICAL FORM

Although the city may not have experienced a major change in physical form under Mu'awiyah, the administrative and political changes that he implemented were to forever change the face of the city under his successors. The innovations of his regime included secularizing the caliphate, changing it into a monarchy, and erecting a throne in the palace for himself. Some of those changes had a symbolic implication for some of the architectural elements that followed.

For example, much of Mu'awiyah's innovations were resented by the Arabs,

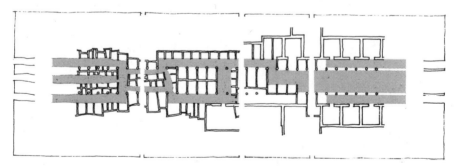

FIGURE 4.9 The Tranformation of the Colonnaded Avenue into the Linear Bazaar of Damascus, Based on Sauvaget.

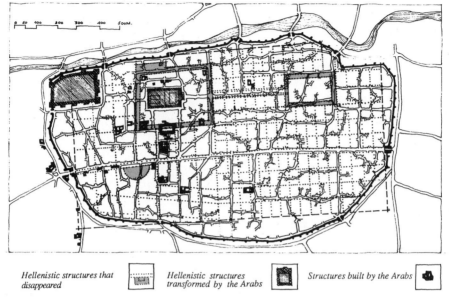

Hellenistic structures that disappeared		Hellenistic structures transformed by the Arabs		Structures built by the Arabs	

FIGURE 4.10   The Street Structure of Damascus during the Ummayad Era, Showing the Transformation. The Outline of the Arab City Overlays the Hellenistic City with its Regular Grid and Major Monuments, Based on Gaube.

and the genuineness of his faith was always challenged. The attempt to assassinate him in the mosque came as no surprise, and his survival brought about the introduction of the *Maqsurah*, an elevated enclosure for the caliph's use during public prayer, as a new important element in mosque architecture.[48]   The significance of the *Maqsurah* lies in the fact that for the first time the caliph stood isolated on a higher level above his subjects, a practice that would have been condemned by the early orthodox caliphs. The *Maqsurah* was an un-Islamic device established for the purpose of maintaining a modified Islamic political system.

It is precisely in this context that we have to analyze the development of Damascus under caliphs Abdul Malek (685–705) and his son al-Walid (705–715).

> *This was the time in which the definite subjugation of Transoxiana was accomplished, the reconquest and pacification of North Africa achieved, and the conquest of Spain undertaken.... Never before and never after did the Syrian capital reach such a peak of power and glory.*[49]

This was also the time in which the Arabization of the state administration was effected. And by the end of the seventh century and during Abdul Malek's administration, Christian officials in the Ummayad court were replaced by Muslim Arab-speaking officials, and freshly minted Arab currency replaced the earlier Byzantine coinage.

Al-Walid's father, Abdul Malek, had his most conspicuous achievements in the field of building great monuments. It was during his reign that the Dome of the Rock and the wall around Damascus were built.[50] Al-Walid followed in his father's footsteps and continued the building tradition by renovating the mosques of Mecca and Madinah. Unlike his predecessors, al-Walid was not content with worshipping in the unpretentious mosque built as part of the space of the Church of St. John and was determined to do something about that.

In his great history of Damascus, Ibn 'Asaker informs us that several caliphs from Mu'awiyah to Abdul Malek had attempted to buy the church from the Christians but were unsuccessful in doing so. Ibn 'Asaker then adds some versions of the story of al-Walid's takeover of the church.[51] The most commonly known story is that the Muslim population of Damascus had increased to the

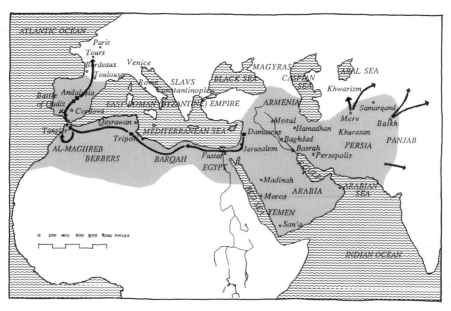

FIGURE 4.11   The Ummayad Empire at Its Height.

extent that it was difficult for them to pray in the mosque on Fridays.

Knowing of this, al-Walid approached the bishop of Damascus with an offer to buy the church and with a warning that refusal of his offer could result in the confiscation and demolition of the church. When the bishop refused to give the church up and instead reminded the caliph of the earlier agreements between the Christians and the Arabs, al-Walid decided to go ahead with his plans.

The three accounts in Ibn 'Asaker agree that the Damascans were reluctant to participate in the takeover of the church because of the popular myth that anyone who demolished the church would go mad. Al-Walid decided to lead the demolition, and Ibn 'Asaker reports that the caliph was the first to climb its tower while declaring, "If in the pursuit of God I have to turn mad, so be it."[52] The Muslim residents of the city were reported to have joined al-Walid in an action that was for many contrary to the essence of Islam and its respect for all religions.

Was the church really demolished instead of being taken over and added to the mosque? This is very unclear. It is possible to view its alleged demolition as a symbolic act announcing the end of the city's Christian era and the beginning of its Islamic one. Watzinger, Walzinger, and Dussaud have all argued that the church was never demolished but was simply taken over, and that the work of al-Walid was confined to the addition of the dome and the remodeling of the church.[53] Taking into consideration all of these theories, Creswell concluded that a church was part of the *temenos* of the temple, or the space which was commonly referred to as the mosque[54] (Refer to **FIGURE 4.5**). In light of the archaeological evidence that supports the inclusion of the church into the mosque, the demolition wrought by al-Walid and his followers may have been confined to the outside envelope of the church. The elimination of its Byzantine image and the eradication of its Christian symbolism paved the way and legitimized the addition of the church space into the expanding mosque.

At whatever cost, al-Walid was determined to build a "great" mosque, unlike any before it. He started first by compensating the Christians through returning to them several churches that had fallen into disuse as a result of the earlier agreements with the Arabs (which had only allowed them to retain certain churches and banned them from using others). Using the service of about 200 skilled craftsmen imported from Byzantium, al-Walid embarked on his ambitious project.[55]

Intent on building a grand building like his father's Dome of the Rock, al-

Walid decided to cover the dome of his new mosque with gold. When he discovered that he could not afford to do so, he substituted gold with lead, another precious metal of his time. But even lead was in short supply, and al-Walid had to request it from Jordan and Egypt. His governor in Jordan was so committed to provide his share of lead that he dug out several Christian graves, which had lead coffins. After reburying the dead, the governor melted the lead and sent it to the caliph in Damascus.[56]

Ibn 'Asaker tells us of another important story regarding the lead shortage during the construction of the Ummayad Mosque. The importance of the story lies in the fact that it reveals al-Walid's inconsistency as a Muslim and contradiction in his personality as a caliph. When lead was in short supply, a Jewish woman was found to be in possession of a considerable amount of the metal. Expecting that al-Walid was going to confiscate the lead as he had earlier confiscated the church, she insisted on selling the lead by weight rather than by volume as was conventional in those days. This meant that the acquisition would have been very expensive. To everyone's surprise, al-Walid ordered his governor to pay the woman all she asked for. Impressed by the caliber of fairness in deciding this matter, she decided not to accept compensation and to give the lead to al-Walid. It is said that in recognition for her gift, the Caliph engraved an acknowledgement to her on one of the lead panels. Ibn 'Asaker reports that the engraving "al-Yahudiah" was still visible in his time.[57]

Why was al-Walid so determined to build such a great mosque? We cannot find a definitive answer to this question. Al-Tabari, al-Baladhri, and Ibn 'Asaker all tell the story that when the Damascans objected to his excessive spending on the mosque, he responded by saying:

> You the people of Damascus take pride in your city because of four things: its air, its water, its fruits and its baths. I wanted to add a fifth item to the things you take pride in.[58]

AN ATTEMPTED RETURN TO ISLAMIC IDEALS

It was not always that Damascus had caliphs who enforced their will and were intent on building the city. In fact, some did not contribute to any building activity, not out of ignorance but out of conviction that the proper Muslim city is a city of faith, not one of buildings. One such caliph was 'Umar ibn Abdul-'Aziz (717–720), the eighth caliph of the Ummayad dynasty, commonly referred to as 'Umar II. When 'Umar II, who was famed for his fairness, took over as caliph, the Christians asked that the Church of St. John be returned to them. They presented the caliph with their earlier agreements with the Arabs, which they felt his fathers and grandfathers had violated by taking over the church. The caliph, who at that time was not living in Damascus, ordered its governor Ibn Suaiyd to return the church to the Christians.[59] If this story is true, it also indicates that the church was not demolished as has been discussed earlier, but that it was rather incorporated into the mosque.

After consulting with the residents of Damascus, who all decided that it was not proper to give up a place where Muslim prayer was constantly held, Ibn Suaiyd agreed to hand back the church on the condition that he be allowed to demolish all the other churches which, according to the earlier treaties the Christians had been citing, were not supposed to be in use. The Christians gave up their demand and decided instead to regain the use of their old churches.[60]

It is interesting that all of this happened under the rule of a caliph called 'Umar II. Like the earlier 'Umar, this caliph was also well known for his modesty and sagacity. During his reign, many of the lavish rituals associated with the caliphate were abandoned. In fact, 'Umar II gave up living in Damascus and moved instead to Der Sama'an, the site of a deserted monastery, where he led an abstemious Sufi life.[61] Again, like the first 'Umar, 'Umar II's zeal as a simple true Muslim was at odds with the state's need to consolidate the Islamic gains. Stories reported about 'Umar II, like the one mentioned above, show the psychological struggle that some of the early Muslim caliphs had to go through before first recognizing Islam's urban dimension and then accepting the inevitable transformation and adaptation of Islamic beliefs for the purpose of defending and promoting the new Islamic empire, or *Dar al-Islam.*

Growing up in the Ummayad palaces, 'Umar II was fully aware of the immense expense involved in their construction and in the construction of mosques like that of Damascus. He realized that such expenses were mainly spent by his predecessors in the spirit of glorifying themselves and not in the service of Islam. In his attempt to enforce a more austere lifestyle, 'Umar II is said to have decided to remove the mosaic and marble tiles and the precious metal decorations of Damascus so as to replace them with other, cheaper materials. 'Amr ibn Muhajer reports hearing the caliph say, "I will sell all these unnecessary items and commit the proceeds to *Baiyt al-Mal* (the Muslim public treasury)."[62]

When the residents of Damascus were informed about the caliph's intent, they were naturally upset. After discussing the matter with their leaders, they sent a delegation headed by Khaled al-'Ashry to dissuade 'Umar II from going ahead with his plans. Whether this delegation was successful in doing so is something that remains unknown. The caliph, however, did change his mind, possibly because of another incident relating to a Byzantine delegation passing through Damascus at that time.

There are actually a number of stories about this delegation, most of which were related by Ibn 'Asaker.[63] The stories center around the delegation's visit to the Mosque of Damascus. After seeking permission to enter, it is reported that they expressed surprise over its grandeur and luxury. The leader of the delegation is reported to have said, "We have always belittled the Arabs and have spoken of their empire as a temporary one! But whoever built this mosque is definitely a great King of a long lasting nation."[64]

Ibn 'Asaker relates that when this incident was reported to the Caliph, he abandoned his plans for the mosque. The incident seems to have convinced 'Umar II that the mosque's lavish appearance, which he was opposing, was in his words a weapon to be used against the enemies of Islam.

This story is of some significance and it should not be dismissed as an admonitory fable designed to justify the opulence of the mosque. It is important because it stands as a turning point in the history of Islamic attitudes toward buildings and cities and because it shows that even a very devout and orthodox caliph, like 'Umar II, was willing to change his mind about what he considered to be the evils of lavish structures and was capable of recognizing that buildings can also have a symbolic value and a political significance. 'Umar II was now recognizing the lesson of his great predecessor, Abul Malek, the builder of the Dome of the Rock. It was now legitimate to build as a means of strengthening the Islamic state.

We have discussed the Arabization of Damascus through telling the stories about the building of its mosque. But the story is not complete without a brief look at another building type, the palaces or the residences where the caliphs lived.

In the early days of Islamic Damascus, few palaces existed in the city proper. Mu'awiyah's palace, which was attached to the Mosque on the *qibla* side, served as a *Dar al-Khalifah* or *Dar al-Malek* (meaning "the residence of the king") and accommodated a few of his successors.[65] 'Umar II seems to have built a residence attached to the northern side of the mosque, and Hisham added another very close by.

It is difficult to know what influenced the early Ummayad Caliphs in their decision to reside in or outside the city. Apparently many of them preferred to live in palaces outside the city. For example, Yazid lived in Hawarin, 'Umar II in Mawaqar, and Hisham in Qasr al-Hayr. This led early scholars such as Von Berchem and Creswell to conclude that the Arabs' nomadic instincts were behind their preference for desert living.[66] The construction of desert palaces or residences may have been a deeply rooted practice in pre-Islamic traditions, but they are of some importance in our attempt to understand the process of assimilation.

Archaeological research has shown that those palaces did not serve only as retreats or hunting lodges for the Ummayad caliphs as the romantic interpretation had it, but also acted as centers of economic development in the now desertified, but in Ummayad times, fertile and highly prosperous arable estates. Obviously many of those palacial compounds consumed more than they produced, but some, like Qasr al-Hayr, were economic enterprises dedicated to agriculture, trade, and settlement purposes.[67] The architecture of these palaces was a continuation of Byzantine patterns, especially in terms of building technology. Although their decoration represented Islamic art at its most nascent stage, their urban symbolism was of limited significance.

In general, the Ummayad caliphs were not interested in using palace buildings to make statements about the Islamic state. And since most of the palaces were not a permanent part of the urban landscape, one may suggest that at least in the case of Damascus, the construction of caliphal palaces was not an act of city building.

Perhaps the story of the transformation of Damascus from a Byzantine to an Arab Muslim city becomes more significant if we know that it was not an exception. That other cities followed the same path mainly signifies the conflict between Arab caliphal authority and Islamic religious ideology. The stories of Aleppo and Cordova under the Ummayads completes the picture drawn by Damascus and exposes the process by which cities were changed under Arab-Muslim rule.

ALEPPO: A PROVINCIAL TOWN

It was in the same year as the fall of Damascus that Arab troops appeared before Aleppo under the command of both Khaled and Abu 'Ubaidah. Unlike Damascus, Aleppo did not have an important administrative or political role in the Byzantine Empire, and its takeover was not considered an event of great

ALEPPO BEFORE ISLAM

1. *Byzantine Cathedral &*
   Episcopal palace
2. *Church*
3. *Synagogue*
4. *Castrum*

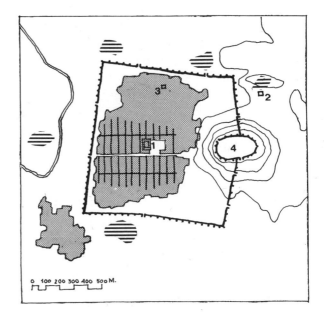

ALEPPO AFTER ISLAM

1. *The Great Mosque*
2. *The Ummayad Mosque*
3. *Musalla*
4. *Fresh produce market*
5. *Citadel*

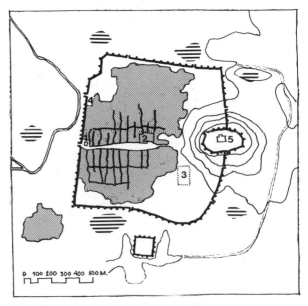

FIGURE 4.12 The Physical Fabric of Aleppo and Its Urban Elements Before and After the Islamic Takeover, Based on Sauvaget.

importance. Like Damascus, Aleppo was a typical Byzantine town with a Greco-Roman grid. The inhabitants of Aleppo seem to have come to an early agreement with the conquerors by which they were required to pay tribute in return for their lives, dwellings and churches.[68]

As they did in Damascus, the Arabs went about searching for a place they could use for their prayers, and again they selected one of the open spaces of the Byzantine city for this purpose. This seems to have been the site of a medieval *largo,* or the space inside the city's western gate. There is no proof that a mosque was ever built there, but the chronicles give several references to this space as a mosque. Sauvaget suggested that the bays of the Byzantine monumental arch which stood at the entrance of the colonnaded street were simply walled in at an early date and used as a mosque.[69] It is difficult to know why the first mosque of Aleppo was located at one end of the city instead of in a more central location, or if, in fact, it ever was a building. One may hypothesize that this space was primarily used as a *musalla,* or a place of prayer during religious festivals. Precedents of a *musalla* close to the gate of the city may be found in Madinah and Damascus.[70] And since the *musalla* was primarily a space and not a building, it is not surprising that the chronicles contain no mention of any dates relating to its establishment. This, however, is rejected by Sauvaget, who suggested a third prayer place or a *musalla* established to the east of the city bulk but still within the wall.

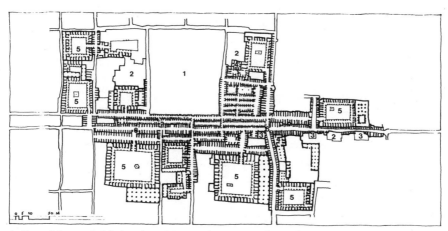

1. Great Mosque 2. Madrasah 3. Mosque 4. Qaiysariyah 5. Khan 6. Colonnaded Street turned Bazaar

FIGURE 4.13 The Bazaar at Aleppo, Growing Over a Grid Pattern, Based on Sauvaget.

The most important mosque in Aleppo does not seem to have appeared until 96/715, close to the end of the first Hijri century. Caliph al-Walid seems to have been responsible for starting construction of this building, which later came to be known as *Masjid al-Jami'*, on the site of the ancient Greek *agora*.[71] The introduction of these three prayer places brought some changes to the land-use pattern and physical fabric of the city[72] (FIGURE 4.12).

In pre-Islamic times, the market occupied part of the former *agora*. But as this later was taken over and made into a mosque, the market had to move out. The fresh-produce market had to move away from the center to a new vacant site within the walled city, leaning against a seldom-used gate. This relocation was a natural move since the market was now brought closer to the fields producing the vegetables and fruits. Markets of more precious goods, like clothing and jewelry, remained at the old site of the *agora*. Thus, in a changing land-use pattern, it became adjacent to the great mosque.[73]

Sauvaget suggested that a new market configuration was needed because the produce market did not provide enough space for all the activities that had previously existed in both the *agora* and the old colonnaded avenue.[74] This came in the form of the *suq*, or the bazaar, with its maze of alleyways, dead-end streets, and courtyards. In the *suq*, a direct and economically profitable use of the old colonnaded avenue was introduced through the rental of spaces and booths to street vendors to set up shop and display goods (FIGURE 4.13).

The transformation of Aleppo seems, then, to have followed a similar pattern to that of Damascus. Many of the earlier Byzantine elements simply disappeared, and a new but still undefined system of urban elements was put in its place. This was the case in the *agora* and the colonnaded avenue, which seem to have been adapted very well to suit the new Arab Muslim functions.

But the lessons of Aleppo are different from those of Damascus. Since Aleppo was not an important city during Umayyad rule, its transformation was more peaceful. For example, the church was not taken over by the Muslims, and the agreement through which the Muslims took over the city included repeated assurances that the church would not be violated.[75] Aleppo also did not contain any major palaces, or at least the chronicles do not give reference to any such building types. That may be due to the fact that Aleppo was part of the *jund*, or administrative unit of Hims and Qinasrin, and that it was not the official residence of any governor.[76]

For a considerable period of time Aleppo possessed only one mosque, located at the western gate. The number of Arabs who moved to the city was small, and it was not until 96/715 that the number had increased to the level that warranted the building of a large mosque.[77] It is also important to note that the mosque of Aleppo was likely initiated during the reign of Caliph al-Walid, the great builder. The decision to build it and the choice of its location — the former *agora* which faced the Byzantine church and acted as its *parvis* — may have been part of al-Walid's undeclared policy of establishing new monuments to symbolize the power of his new rising Islamic Empire.

Aleppo confirms that the transformation of provincial towns taken over by the Arabs was slightly different from that of the capital. It does not, however, minimize the importance of caliphal authority in bringing about this transformation. Establishing an Islamic urban image for Aleppo as a provincial city may not have been on the caliphs' agenda, but it eventually happened when function dictated it.

CORDOVA: THE ARABIZATION OF A MEDIEVAL EUROPEAN CITY

It was during the Ummayad rule that the Arab invasion of Visigothic Spain was achieved. By 92/711 the forces of Tareq ibn Ziyad and Musa ibn Nusaiyr managed to take over the bulk of the Iberian Peninsula in less than seven years, and for the first time in Islam's history, a major military victory was achieved using an army of Berber converts.[78] The events on the Ummayad mainland detracted attention from this major drive to Islamize the West. This corresponded to the time when the Ummayad dynasty was fighting for its life.

Initially the Arabs chose Seville as their provincial capital, but during the first decade, the Ummayad governor, al-Samh ibn Malek, transferred the seat to Cordova. Little Arab immigration to Spain was reported during this early era, and except for the presence of some Muslim garrisons, we know very little about how and where the Arabs lived.[79] The event that helped populate the cities of Spain occurred a few years later in 132/750 with the Abbasid revolution and the fall of the Ummayad dynasty.[80]

The anti-Ummayad movement, which started in Khurasan, an Ummayad province in eastern Persia, and gained ground with the call to proclaim Abu al-Abbas as a new caliph who would enforce a return to Islamic ideals, culminated in the Ummayad defeat and the complete massacre of the Ummayad royal family.[81] The dramatic escape of the nineteen-year-old Ummayad prince Abdul Rahman was to change the face of the Islamic empire for years to follow.

Abdul Rahman fled first to North Africa and from there to Spain, where he quickly established himself as governor. The following year he discontinued mention of the Abbasid name in the Friday *khutbah*, or sermon, and declared Spain an independent emirate.[82] At first Abdul Rahman was faced with enormous problems. The dual character of the Spanish population, with its Christian-Muslim polarization, the conflict between the Shiites and the Sunnites, the feuds between the Arabs and the Berbers who helped invade Spain, were some of his problems. Pursuing a policy of tolerance, Abdul Rahman attempted to mediate between those different groups with their varying interests and outlook on life.[83]

In Cordova, Abdul Rahman set up a government that was administratively modeled after that of his ancestors in Damascus, but adapted it to local needs and held all military and political authority. Abdul Rahman also maintained the Visigothic provincial divisions, assigning to each a *wali*, or governor, to take care of local financial and military affairs, and a *qadi*, or judge, to handle the religious and legal matters.

Since Spain was Christianized relatively late, it was not difficult for the Arabs to embark on its Islamization. By embracing Islam, large numbers of the discontented Visigothic servile class and slaves were set free, and several important Visigothic families adopted Islam to seek relief from the Kharaj and Jeziah taxes.[84]

During the early Arab occupation, few changes occurred in Cordova, a typical medieval European city. As in Damascus, the Arabs simply occupied vacant houses while the economic and business activity continued to be conducted as before. But when Abdul Rahman took over, there was a need to symbolize the new Arab state, and Cordova, his political capital, had to become a religious capital. And so it was that the earlier Roman temple, which by the time of the conquest was a Visigothic cathedral, was selected by Abdul Rahman to be converted into a mosque in 167/785.

Before starting this magnificent project, which took almost 100 years to complete, Abdul Rahman embarked on an ambitious construction program that included religious and secular buildings. This inspiration may have come from his predecessors, the builders of the earliest monumental structures of Islam.[85] In addition to building his famous Al-Rusafah palace outside Cordova, Abdul Rahman has been credited with improving the infrastructure of the city by means of public-works projects that included aqueducts, bridges, and fortifications.

Ibn 'Udhri and al-Maqri, the main sources on the history of the Cordova mosque, tell us very little about how the church or cathedral was converted into a mosque. They both, however, agree that the Arabs acted on the precedent set by Khaled ibn al-Walid, following the capture of Damascus in which part of the church was taken over and transformed into a mosque.[86]

Since we have already established the unlikelihood of the Damascus church's ever being divided and used simultaneously as a church and a mosque, it makes no sense to try to challenge the validity of these stories. Creswell had suggested that it was the traveler Ibn Jubaiyr who brought the Damascus legend back to Spain. There it became popularized and probably linked to the Cordova mosque to the extent that it later got incorporated into several reputable chronicles, including those of Ibn Udhri and al-Maqri.[87]

It is possible, though, that the church may not have been converted into a mosque, but that the open space in front of it or around it was simply used as a space for prayer by the Muslims. In fact, some chronicles contain reference to a *musalla* space alongside the church in the early days.[88] If this is true, then the pattern established in Damascus appears to have been repeated in Cordova.

If one also considers what happened to the caliphal palace in Cordova, another pattern inherited from Damascus becomes clear, even though here it takes a different dimension. As the Ummayad dynasty in Spain was growing older, the caliph, by that time Abdul Rahman III, decided to move out of Cordova. He selected for his new residence al-Zahrah, a site outside the city in the Sierra Morena, and then spent close to twenty-five years building it.[89] Unlike the Ummayad palaces in Syria, this new caliphal court was designed to impress. In it the caliph had planned to receive the envoys of the monarchs of Europe; unlike the simple Arab *majlis*, or court, this was a place to display not only Arab hospitality but also Arab power.

By then, it was almost one hundred years since the death of Muhamad, and the Arabs seem to have come to the conclusion that to Islamize the West they have to behave like westerners. Over successive generations, their caliphs had finally realized that Islam's simple nature as a religion did not provide them with enough means to satisfy their ambitions as monarchs. To legitimize their image-building, they had to seek a reinterpretation of Islam's attitude toward the construction of great monuments. Now a lavish mosque and a lavish caliphal court were accepted not as legitimate ends but as means to spread the word of Allah and consolidate the power of the caliph.

THE TRANSFORMATION OF EXISTING TOWNS

Based on the above explanations of the cases of Damascus, Aleppo, and Cordova, it is possible to say that the Arab Muslim appropriation of the urban fabric seems to have followed a consistent pattern. The process began by taking over some open space close to an existing building like a temple, church, or a gate within the town. The selected space served as a place for public prayers. Most of these spaces, however, usually accommodated some pre-Islamic function, like commercial exchange or religious festivities. (We cannot find enough evidence to support the popular notion that those spaces disappeared when the functional needs for them ceased to exist.) The process continued as more conversions occurred and the Muslim population of the town grew and the need to make this space into a building arose. Once built, this mosque took over the functional dominance of the church, or cathedral, and with time commands the urban scene. Finally, as the Muslims became more powerful and more in control, they appropriated the church. This was accomplished through negotiations at the end of which the church was usually bought or taken over by force. The church was then demolished or simply incorporated into the structure that eventually became the central mosque of the town.

A parallel pattern regarding the residence of the caliph or amir may be observed. At first an existing structure was taken over and designated as *Dar al-Khilafah* or *Dar al-Imarah*. This was usually remodeled, renovated, or completely reconstructed so as to display its strong physical connection to the mosque. Finally, this palace was abandoned as the caliph or the amir moved to the outskirts of the town or outside it altogether, and built himself a palatial compound.

As far as existing evidence seems to indicate, the early mosques and palaces were not very distinguished as buildings and they did not seem to have the appearance of monuments with any symbolic statements.[90] The first element to ever achieve an Islamic symbolic significance may have been the minaret of the Ummayad mosque in Damascus, although its addition is likely to have occurred at a later date. When the church was taken over and transformed into a mosque, the corner tower of the Roman *temenos* was incorporated into it and used by the Mu'azen for the Call for Prayer. It is ironic that all of this occurred at a time when the city was still predominantly Christian, leading Grabar to conclude that the minaret was remodeled as part of the mosque not so much for its technical function but rather as a symbolic expression of the presence of the new religion directed towards the non-Muslim population of the city.[91]

Although much of this transformational pattern in existing cities was accidental, one can still identify elements of an unselfconscious program put in place by the caliphs and the amirs to bring about the conversion of the city fabric at the same time that the conversion of the population was under way. The chronicles, for example, contain frequent references to what the natives were allowed to do or were banned from doing following the Arab occupation of Damascus. Christians were given the freedom of worship and were allowed to ring their church bells.[92] They were, however, forbidden to ride horses inside the city. This, of course, was part of a latent Arab policy intent on suppressing the Christians.

Although it was against the spirit of true Islam, denying the Christians some of their civil rights and political freedom was a means of enforcing Arab superiority. It is clear that at this early stage the conquerors were still fighting for the honor and glory of their big Arab tribe and that the religious ideals of the Islamic religion had to be set aside so that they could establish their new Arab empire.

I started this chapter with the goal of trying to discover how the cities that predated Islam developed when they were taken over by the Muslim Arabs. Most of my concern has been with ways that they were Arabized or Islamized. But what the last few pages have tried to show is that the Arabs, themselves, were also changing. They were heading in a direction different from that envisioned by Muhamad and his orthodox followers. Changes in Arab mentality brought changes in the form of existing cities. These changes were not representations of Islamic ideology but indirect reflections of the changing order of Arab Muslim society.

V

PLANNED CAPITAL CITIES
IDEAL CONSTRUCTS OR IMPERIAL PALACES

> *The Arab conquests did not introduce urbanity. . . [but]*
> *they entailed the formation of new empires which had*
> *their own reasons for city construction. The Caliphs and*
> *governors built new capitals to. . . symbolize the domi-*
> *nance of a particular regime or ruler and his capacity to*
> *bring order and civilization to his domain.*[1]
> IRA LAPIDUS

Most scholars of Islamic urbanism recognize the existence of two distinct types of settlements: the planned and the spontaneous. Under this classification, garrison towns such as Basrah and Kufah are not considered planned settlements because their form was a result of the rapid spontaneous growth that accompanied the Islamic expansion.[2] Accordingly, all such garrison towns are unfortunately dismissed as examples of Arab Muslim town planning, creating a situation in which capital towns like Baghdad or Cairo are left as the only true representatives of Islamic planning concepts.

Earlier, I have attempted to show that although garrison towns were not based on a preconceived plan, they were, nevertheless, a clear and honest representation of a variety of Arab planning ideals derived from the Islamic religion. In this chapter I will explore the other notion that capital towns were conceived as ideal Islamic towns and that their plans reveal much about the symbolism of the Islamic system. Whereas Damascus and Cordova and the decisions that shaped their form were representative of the struggle between forces seeking to glorify Islam and those simply seeking to enforce its ideals, capital cities such as Baghdad and Cairo were simply products of a single individual's will. The forms of such cities, which we try to study here by concentrating on the Arab chronicles, were mainly a reflection of an imperial authority that had little to do with Islamic urban ideals. Demonstrating this point may allow us to challenge the idea of a stereotypical Arab Muslim city from another direction.

To understand all of this, we have to place it in its actual historic context. Close to the middle of the eighth century, the Ummayad dynasty was folding down. When Marwan II took over as Caliph in 126/744, the Ummayad empire, which by now extended from the Atlantic to the borders of China, was internally torn by innumerable problems. Among these were the constant feuds between the Ummayad family and their arch-enemies from old times, the Alids and the Kharijites, and the discontent of the non-Arab Muslims.[3]

Since the civil war between Ali and Muawiyah, the Muslim world had been divided in two: the followers of the Ummayads who were called Sunnis, on the one hand, and the Alids, or the partisans of the descendants of Ali, who later became known as Shiites, on the other hand. The Alids were by now very vocal in opposing the legitimacy of the Ummayad caliphate. The problems of the Ummayads were further complicated by the reappearance of two other groups: the puritan Kharijites, who were now trying to establish themselves in North Africa, and the old Quraishi clan, the Abbasids, who were blood relatives of the prophet and whose claims for leadership had hitherto been represented by the Alids.[4]

The revolt against the Ummayads started in Persia where the great numbers of the people who had converted to Islam were still deprived of the right to be exempt from the poll tax required of all non-Muslim Arabs. Under the leadership of Abu Muslim, the rebels allied themselves with the Abbasid family, whose propaganda machine had brought discontent among the Persians by alleging the overworldliness of the Ummayads.[5] After establishing headquarters in Merv, the rebels passed triumphantly into Persia, occupying Kufah in 131/749. Muhamad ibn abu al-Abbas, the head of the Abbasid clan, whose nickname was "Al-Saffah," or "the blood shedder," seized the opportunity to proclaim himself the rightful caliph — to the dismay of some of his Shiite supporters, who were more interested in the appointment of someone from the Alid family.

A few months later, the Ummayad caliph was defeated in a battle on the banks of the river Zab and the forces of the Abbasids occupied Damascus, massacred the Ummayad family, and chased its last caliph, Marwan II, to Egypt, where they assassinated him. The battle of Zab was one of the most decisive battles in this history of Islamic civilization, for it resulted in the orientalization of Islam.[6] The empire, which up to now had been breathing from the Medi-

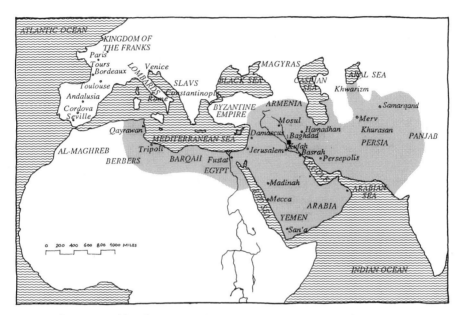

FIGURE 5.1   The Abbasid Empire (136/754).

terranean, was now turning to the East to reestablish itself (**FIGURE 5.1**).

With the help of the experienced Persians, the Abbasids rapidly set out to provide the empire with an effective central administration.[7] They moved the seat of government from Damascus to al-Hashimiyah on the outskirts of Kufah, shifting the center of power eastward and leaving Arabia as well as Syria out of focus.[8]

A New Dynasty and a New Capital

The first Abbasid caliph, al-Saffah, did not reign long enough to enjoy his triumph. When he died in 136/754, he was succeeded by his brother, Abu Ja'afar, who was acclaimed as al-Mansur, or the victorious caliph.[9] Mistrusting the inhabitants of Kufah, which was overrun by the Alids, al-Mansur desired to move closer to Persia, where his main support base was located.[10] The attempt by the Rawandiyah, an extremist proto-Shiite sect, on al-Mansur's life in Kufah convinced him of the need to establish a new capital.[11]

Al-Tabari relates that al-Mansur had no intention of leaving the choice of a locality for his new city to chance. He undertook the task of identifying the site himself. It took almost four years before the site was determined and construction of its major buildings began in 145/762.[12]

In determining the site, al-Mansur searched as far north as Musul without finding anything specific to his liking. But two earlier localities had attracted his attention. The first was the village of Jarjaiya on the Tigris, close to the ancient twin capital Seleucia-Ctesiphon. The second was the village of Baghdad, situated at a point where the old Sarat Canal joined the Tigris.[13]

Historians gave a variety of reasons for al-Mansur's choice of site. Some of these may go beyond rationalized historical facts into legend, but if all of them are true they may stand as an indication of al-Mansur's complex personality. One of those functional aspects behind the choice of the site has been attributed to its climatic suitability. After deciding on a general area within which the new capital would achieve central location, al-Mansur summoned the heads of the Christian villages and monasteries in the area. He questioned them about the attributes of their sites with regard to heat, cold, rain, mud, and mosquitoes. Not content with that, he gave orders to various members of his retinue to go to those villages, spend the night there, and bring back a detailed report on their experiences. After reviewing the reports, al-Mansur chose the site of Baghdad.[14]

It seems that the choice of a site that was the meeting place of caravan routes in a fertile plain with its net of water canals was a logical one.[15] But all those functional factors should not lead us to dismiss some of the other stories regarding the choice of the site that may be classified as legends or myths.

One such story, reported in different chronicles with some variation, concerns an incident encountered by one of the caliph's entourage who was forced to remain behind because of illness while the search for the capital site was taking place.[16] The physician who treated him, who in some accounts was also a monk, pointed to a prophecy in his own local tradition which said that only a man called Miqlas would build a great city on a site between the Tigris and the Sarat Canal. The implication of the physician's advice was that al-Mansur was wasting his time searching for a site there since his name was not Miqlas.[17]

When the caliph was informed of the incident, it is reported that he was very touched since he recalled that in his childhood he was indeed nicknamed Miqlas. This seems to have added to his determination to select the site of Baghdad. Jacob Lassner, who has studied this incident, concluded that the story was cited by various historians not only because it satisfied ancient expectations but also because it offered current proof of al-Mansur's legitimacy to rule.[18]

THE SHAPE OF BAGHDAD AND THE BUILDING PROCESS

After consulting with his astrologers, al-Mansur immediately started construction on the selected site. He brought together engineers, builders, and surveyors from many parts of the empire and described to them his plan for a city having a circular shape with his palace and mosque at its center.[19] Estimates of the city size range from .5 million to 64 million square cubits. Most historians, however, seem to accept a report claimed to have been related by Rabah, the architect of the city wall, which gave a measurement for the circumference that translates into a city diameter of around 2,500 meters or 8,250 feet.[20]

We know very little about how the plan was conceptualized or if a drawing of it was made. Yaqubi mentions that the city plan was traced during the reign of al-Saffah.[21] Since he gave no details and since he does not use the word *Ikhtat*, it is difficult for us to use this piece of information to understand the plan. Al-Tabari explains that al-Mansur wanted to visualize what the city would look like if built, so he ordered that the plan be traced on the ground with lines of ashes; he then entered the city from its to-be gates and walked around. As he reached the center he ordered the placement of cotton seeds saturated with a flammable liquid on the traced lines and set fire to it.[22] This supposedly enabled the caliph to see and sense the form of his city before its foundations were dug.

According to al-Tabari, the caliph then selected a group of honest and virtuous men, including legal scholars, theologians, and religious leaders, to participate in the erection of the city, or what he referred to as *handasah*.[23] The use of the word *handasah* here is of some significance. In contemporary Arabic, *handasah* means "engineering," and its use by al-Tabari indicates al-Mansur's desire to give religious legitimacy to his act of building by including religious scholars in his team of architects and engineers. Among those asked to participate in the construction was Abu Hanifah, the famed theologian and founder of the Hanafi rite, who seems to have reluctantly accepted the task.[24]

The construction of Baghdad did not go very smoothly, and al-Mansur was forced to halt it several times to suppress a rebellion in Madinah and to crush the Alid uprising in Kufah. When construction was restarted, a search for building materials was initiated to replace the wood, metal and equipment intentionally burnt or destroyed in fear that the Alids' would win the war and overtake the site.[25]

As customary of new regimes, al-Mansur decided to use the building materials of a nearby ruined Sassanian palace at al-Mada'in or Ctesiphon.[26]

When his main counsellor, Khaled ibn Barmak, argued that preserving the ruined palace represents a better use of the materials since it stands as a reminder of the Muslim triumph over the Persians, the caliph accused him of pro-Persian sentiments stemming from his national Iranian origin. After ordering the demolition, the venture proved to be uneconomical as salvage costs were discovered to be very expensive. Al-Mansur then abandoned the demolition again at the objection of his counsellor, who now reversed himself to argue that terminating the project would reduce the caliph's status in the eyes of his subjects and appear as admission of his inability to destroy a symbol of Sassanian rule.[27]

Since excavations on the presumed site of Baghdad have never revealed much, all discussions of its plan must rely upon the literary descriptions in the chronicles of al-Baghdadi, al-Tabari, and al-Ya'aqubi. From those sources we know that the city was divided into three concentric zones. At the center was the *rahbah*, or the main space within which the palace of the caliph, the congregational mosque, and some other minor buildings were located. In the second zone, the ring surrounding the *rahbah*, were palaces for the younger sons of al-Mansur and some of his government agencies. In the third zone, the outer

FIGURE 5.2 (ABOVE AND FACING PAGE) Two Views of a General Reconstruction of Baghdad as Initially Planned by al-Mansur.

ring, there were the residences of the caliph's army chiefs and some of their soldiers. The city was walled and had four gates, each with an arcaded street connecting it to the *rahbah* and thus dividing the city into four quadrants. Within each quadrant, al-Mansur estimated areas for shops and markets and instructed the engineers to make street widths fifty cubits (23 meters or 75 feet) and lane widths sixteen cubits (7 meters or 24 feet)[28] (FIGURE 5.2).

Before construction was finished, the markets were relocated to each of the four arcades leading from the gates to the *rahbah*.[29] According to Creswell, the city was surrounded from outside by a moat or a ditch which was crossed over by four bent entrances, forming the four gates of the city, which in turn carried the names of cities they faced.[30]

Al-Mansur called his city Madinat al-Salam, or the City of Peace. There are many explanations for the reasons behind giving the city this name, which was often used concurrently with its general name Baghdad.[31] Perhaps it is relevant for us to concentrate on the reasons behind its round form. In his *The Shaping of Abbasid Rule*, Lassner reviews all the different theories about the circular form of the city. The most important is that which perceives the form as a representation of a cosmic order. Protagonists of this view see the plan as really nothing less than an Islamic *mandala* that implied a schematic representation of the world derived from pre-Islamic Persian and Indian precedents.

Although Lassner warns against the cosmological analysis, he nevertheless does not dismiss it. He draws attention to several factors discussed also by others. Among these were al-Mansur's fear for his personal safety, which prompted him to consider isolating himself in the center and surrounding his palace by an open space controlled by his bodyguards.[32] The round shape, the most convenient for defense purposes,[33] was also perceived as a just form, for it allowed the different sections of the city to exist equidistant from his palace.[34] The most plausible explanation for the shape, however, is that al-Mansur simply followed ancient Parthian-Sassanian precedents for building a military camp according to a circular form.[35] Like Lassner, I will not dismiss the cosmological analogy, well argued by some contemporary scholars.[36] I only suggest that it should be seen in the context of the Arabs' knowledge and acceptance of many outside influences and foreign concepts. To al-Mansur, especially in the early

---

1. Caliphal Palace 2. Mosque 3. Rahbah 4. Markets 5. Palaces of the Royal Family 6. Residential Quarters 7. Gates 8. River & Canals

FIGURE 5.3 (FACING PAGE) The General Site Arrangement of Baghdad and Its Urban Elements.

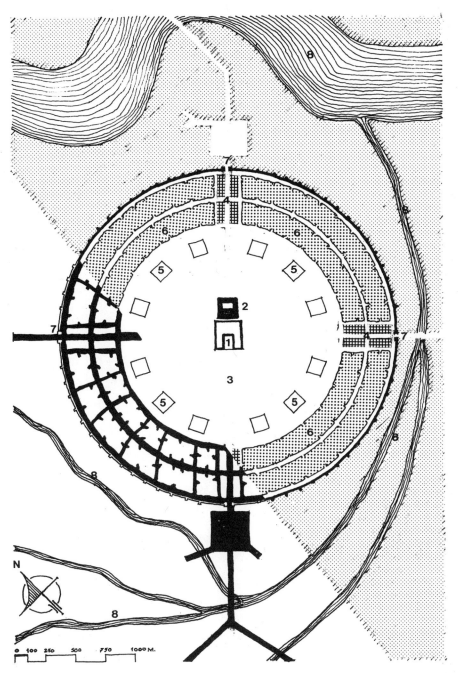

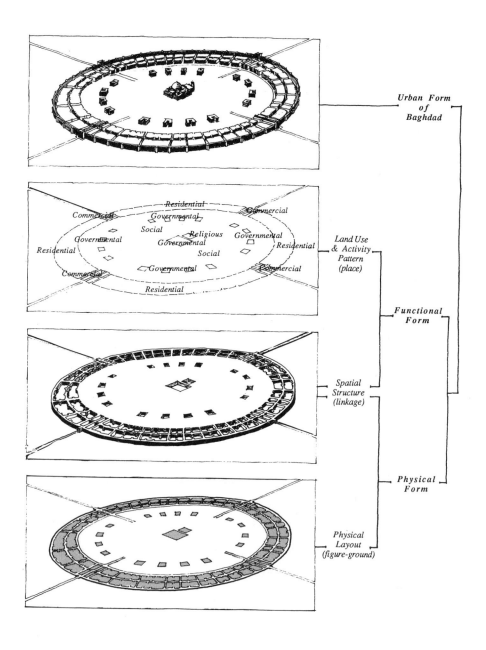

FIGURE 5.4 The Initial Urban Form of Baghdad Analyzed.

days, Baghdad may have simply represented an imperial palace from which he would rule.

THE MAIN ELEMENTS OF THE CAPITAL

The elements making up Madinat al-Salam were fairly distinct: a major palace, a congregational mosque, a few public buildings, a few smaller palaces, a few scattered markets, and a concentric zone of residential quarters (FIGURES 5.3 and 5.4).

The palace occupied the center of the city. Referred to as the Palace of the Golden Gate, it was a square-shaped building with sides measuring 400 cubits (182 meters or 500 feet) each. In it there was a tunnel-vaulted iwan looking into the caliph's audience room, or *majlis*, which in turn was covered by an 80-cubit- (36 meters or 120 feet) high green dome, reminiscent of that of Mu'awiyah's palace in Damascus.[37] The mosque was attached to the palace and occupied an area that was no more than one-quarter of that of the palace. The original structure was made of sun-dried bricks set in clay with a roof supported on wooden columns.[38] The plan of the mosque was very simple and followed the early prototype of Madinah, having a central courtyard. In later days, when the number of worshippers increased, the mosque was enlarged by the addition of another courtyard and the structures around it. There are many theories about how this was achieved, but most agree that the enlargement was accomplished through the takeover of either part of the palace or a neighboring building, also attached to the palace, which was called *Dar al-Qattan*. Herzfeld, Creswell, and Lassner attempted different reconstructions of the relationship between the mosque and the palace (FIGURE 5.5). Regardless of which reconstruction is more accurate, it appears likely that the mosque and the palace may not have been initially conceived as one complex by their creator as many scholars have suggested, but rather that the mosque was simply an addition to the palace, even though this situation may have changed in later times.

The mosque and palace stood at the center of the *rahbah*, or the great open plaza. Surrounding them were a few houses built by al-Mansur for his sons and army chiefs. This seems to have formed an inner ring around the city. Beyond this, the outer ring contained the residential quarters mentioned earlier. Vaulted arcades ran from the main gate to the palace area and were transferred to act as markets before construction of the city was finished[39] (FIGURE 5.6).

According to al-Ya'aqubi, the quarters inside the outer ring were divided into *sikak*, or lanes. Each *sikah* was designated as a residence for an army chief

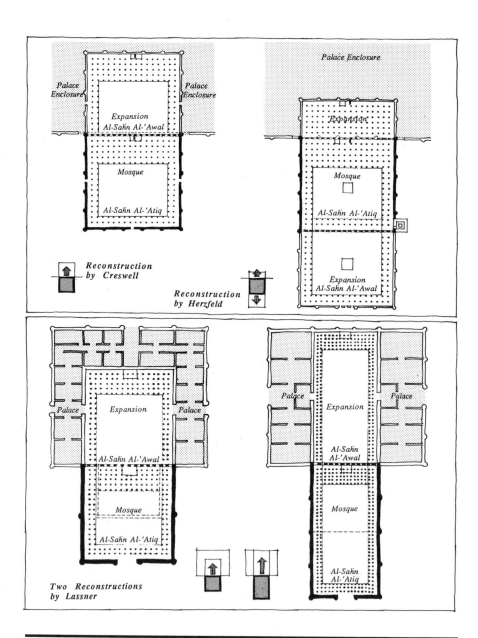

FIGURE 5.5 The Different Reconstructions of the Relationship Between the Mosque and the Palace of al-Mansur in the Round City, According to Creswell, Herzfeld and Lassner.

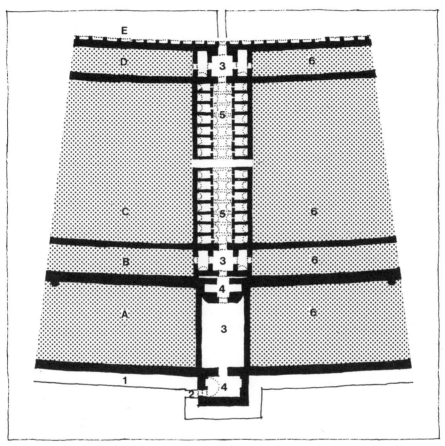

1. Moat (Khandaq) 2. Bridge 3. Rahbah 4. Dahliz 5. Taqat (Commercial bays)
6. Residential Quarters A. First Zone (Guards) B. Second Zone C. Residential Quarters
D. Third Zone (Public officials) E. Caliph's Royal Space

FIGURE 5.6 Creswell's Reconstruction of the *Taqat* or the Vaulted Arcades that Accommodated the Early Markets.

and his soldiers. The two ends of each *sikah* were gated and closed with doors at night and opened in the morning to the ring street.[40] Al-Baghdadi describes the houses as being connected and abutting each other.[41]

The organization of those various elements on the plan is very crucial to an understanding of its significance and symbolism. Perhaps the true significance of Baghdad lies not so much in the physical character of its forms as in the ideas suggested by the forms.[42] The green dome in the middle was very symbolic. Although its color and name were not innovative (for they had existed in Ummayad times), it clearly stood as a symbol of imperial authority.

The organization of the different elements on site has also been subject to a variety of graphic interpretations (FIGURE 5.7). LeStrange's reconstruction of 1900, for example, placed the mosque to the southeast of the palace and scattered the different palatial and public buildings in the central space.[43] Working a few years later, Herzfeld placed the mosque southwest of the palace, arguing that the renovation that took place in it later in relation to the palace could only have happened if it were located on this side. Citing earlier precedents in which the caliph or the amir was usually given direct access from his palaces to the *maqsura*, Creswell suggested that the mosque must have adjoined the palace from the northeast side, thus creating a situation in which the *qibla* wall of the mosque was in direct contact with the palace.[44] Since this was also the case in Kufah, Basrah, and Damascus, Creswell's plan gains more legitimacy and has been adopted by most scholars.[45] Lassner's plan, however, remains the most accurate, for he adds the configuration of the inner ring and, through a comparative examination of the descriptions in the Chronicles, arrives at the conclusion that only two other security buildings existed within the *rahbah*.[46]

Regardless of these variations in the placement of elements of the plan, we may be justified in suggesting that in the case of Baghdad, what mattered, at least in the conceived plan, was the idea of centrality. The circular shape transformed this carefully mapped palatial compound into an unselfconscious attempt to make an entity that would symbolize the total rule and universal legitimacy of the caliph.

BAGHDAD: IMMEDIATE CHANGES IN FORM

Changes in the circular form of the city of al-Mansur started even before the first stage of construction was finished, although the round city is said to have preserved some of its shape for some years thereafter.[47] The workers engaged in the construction of the city were housed outside, and as the inner part started to take some shape, the outer one was already developing rapidly.

In describing the organization of the city's neighborhoods, al-Ya'aqubi makes a clear distinction between those located within the city wall and those outside it. He mentions that al-Mansur gave orders to make *sikak*, or streets, and *durub*, or thoroughfares extending from the city to these *rabads*, or outer

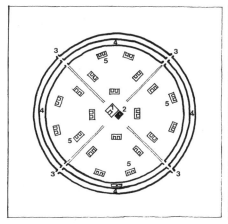

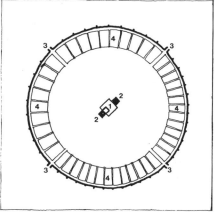

RECONSTRUCTION BY LeStrange
1. Caliphal Palace 2. Mosque 3. Gates
4. Residential Quarters 5. Palaces of the
Royal Family

RECONSTRUCTION BY
CRESWELL & HERZFELD
1. Caliphal Palace 2. Mosque 3. Gates
4. Residential Quarters

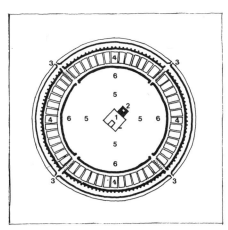

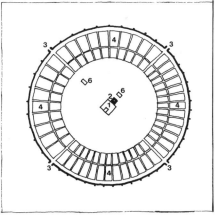

RECONSTRUCTION BY HITTI
1. Caliphal Palace 2. Mosque 3. Gates
4. Residential Quarters 5. Palaces of the
Royal Family 6. Government Offices

RECONSTRUCTION BY LASSNER
1. Caliphal Palace 2. Mosque 3. Gates
4. Residential Quarters 6. Government Offices

FIGURE 5.7 The Different Reconstruction of the Plan of Baghdad and the Location of Its Urban Elements, According to LeStrange, Creswell, Herzfeld, Hitti and Lassner.

quadrants. Al-Mansur then granted several of those areas to some of his relatives, his army chiefs, or to a group of people from a certain country. Those quarters and their *darbs* or lanes were named after their respective groups. Much of this property seems to have been granted by al-Mansur in the form of *qata'ia*, or fiefs, to specific well known individuals.[48] In describing the development outside the wall, al-Ya'qubi starts from the gates and moves outward, making it very explicit that he was describing an area outside the round city, although some scholars have interpreted this to be the outer ring. This had led many to the belief that the circular city was only a palace precinct rather than an integrated city.[49]

It is difficult for us here to judge the nature of the relationship between the round city and its surroundings. This could be done only if we were to pay some additional attention to the changes that happened in regard to the other functional elements, like the markets, the administrative quarters, and the caliphal palace.

Al-Mansur did not initially plan to have a centralized market with specialized bazaars in his circular city.[50] The four arcades leading from the gates at the outside wall to the *rahbah*, which were designated to accommodate the markets seem not to have been enough.[51] The increasing number of the population, the large amount of money distributed among them, the rise of their purchasing power and standard of living, and the great demand for laborers and craftsmen seem to have brought about the need to transfer the markets outside the circular city.[52]

No one can pin down the exact reason for the transfer of the markets. Al-Khatib informs us that in the year 157/773, al-Mansur ordered the market transfer to al-Karkh, an area to the south of the round city[53] (Refer to FIGURE 5.9). In al-Tabari, al-Khatib, and Yaqut, we find variations of the story of the Byzantine ambassador who on visiting the city brought to the caliph's attention the danger posed by the proximity of the markets. Patrikios, the ambassador, seems to have pointed out that the enemy might enter the city under the guise of carrying out trade and that the merchants in turn could pass on vital information about the caliph's activities to outsiders.[54] This may have convinced the caliph to order the relocation of the market in an attempt to free the city from all activities unnecessary to him.

Al-Mansur became convinced that the architectural arrangement he originally envisioned was not necessarily in his best security interest. The earlier inconveniences about the market seem to have also convinced him of the need to isolate himself even more, and to establish the *rahbah* as a purely imperial

STAGE I

The caliph's earlier personal domain with major functions overlooking the Rahbah.

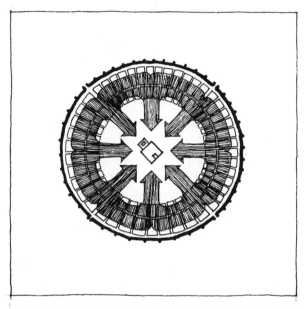

STAGE 2

The caliph's introverted personal domain, after the surrounding buildings were separated from the space by a wall.

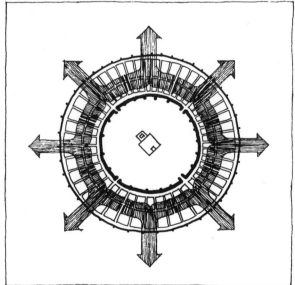

FIGURE 5.8   The Transformation of the Central Space into a Caliphal Private Domain.

domain. Accordingly, he gave orders to the people living in the inner ring of the city to shift the portals that opened onto the *rahbah* so that they faced the outside perimeters instead[55] (FIGURE 5.8). These changes redefined the function of the palace complex. The caliph's domain was thus limited to the great central court with his residence, his mosque, and the buildings for his guards. As before, this area was only accessible by passing through the stringent security checks within the small arcades.[56]

How could the city have functioned in this manner is unknown to us. If the people were allowed to use the mosque for their Friday prayer, would this not have constituted a breach of al-Mansur's alleged desire for security? Was the market so weak an institution that it could be relocated twice with no serious repercussions or objections? How did the people of Baghdad feel when they had to leave their walled city to buy some of their daily goods from outside? Many of those questions will have to remain unanswered because the Arab chronicles seem to have concentrated more on the caliph's actions as a way of documenting the history of the city than on the feelings of ordinary people who lived in it.

In the end, al-Mansur's attempts to control the city and ensure his personal security proved unmanageable. He started by relocating some of his troops to the left bank of the river Tigris to an area that became known as al-Rusafah after a palace he built for his son al-Mahdi, whom he asked to move there.[57] It is interesting to note here that al-Mansur also built two mosques in each of these two developing suburbs of the city: the Karkh, which accommodated the markets on the south, and al-Rusafah, which accommodated the troops and al-Mahdi's palace to the northeast. In doing so the caliph was making it more convenient for the residents of those sections to have their Friday prayers close by, and he was also ensuring a lesser crowd and probably a more manageable situation in his central mosque (FIGURE 5.9).

But the caliph ultimately gave it all up. The circumstances leading to his abandoning the round city are not very clear, and it seems that his perception of the city as an unsafe architectural trap was behind his decision to build himself a new

---

1. Caliphal Palace 2. Mosque 3. Old Markets 4. New Market at Al-Karakh 5. Al-Khuld Palace 6. New Friday Mosque 7. Mahdi's Rusafah Palace 8. The Palace of Al-Mu'tasim 9. Al Firdus Palace

FIGURE 5.9 (FACING PAGE) The Developments Outside the Round City, Showing the Relocation of the Markets in al-Karakh and the New Mosques and Palaces Built by al-Mansur and his Immediate Successors, Based on LeStrange.

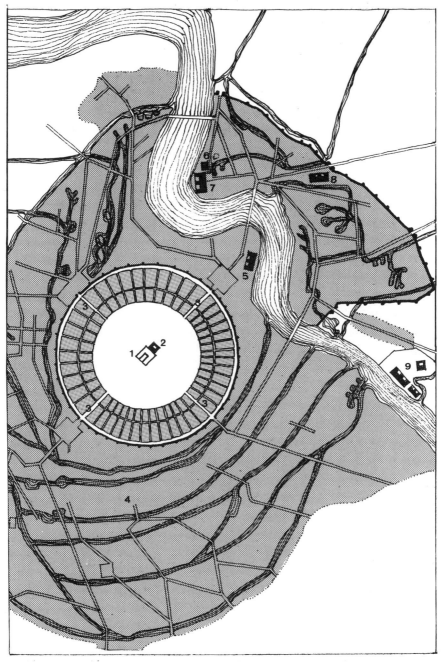

residence, the palace of al-Khuld, situated along the Tigris to the northeast of the Khurasan gate.[58] The palace of al-Khuld was not simply a new residence, but part of a delicate compromise by which the caliph hoped to retain the official image established earlier by the palace of the Golden Gate without duplicating any of the features of the round city.[59] Government agencies, however, started springing up around the new palace, splitting forever the centrality and self-containment of the government complex established in the round city.

The palace of al-Khuld was later to become the official residence for many of the Abbasid caliphs, and from that point on it was clear that the round city was no longer a city but simply a neighborhood in greater Baghdad. Development of this larger urban region was happening concurrently with the caliph's building projects (Refer to FIGURE 5.9). The extent of the development outside the round city gives support to the view that the city grew from outside, since many of the surrounding neighborhoods started to flourish even before construction of the round city was completed.

Baghdad's urban institutions developed in parallel to its physical form. However, we know very little about the development of these institutions. Such institutions included *Diwan al-Nazar fi al-Mazalem*, or the bureau of complaints, the *wizarah*, or the body of advisers, and the position of *qadi al-qudat*, or the chief justice. These all seem to have been institutions associated with the functions of the caliphate and with the activities of Baghdad as a capital. City institutions included the positions of the *muhtasib*, *'amil al-suq*, the market supervisor, the *saheb al-Shurtah*, chief of police, the *talifa*, the guilds, and the *shaikhs*, the leaders of the residential quarters.[60]

In the early days there was no clear distinction between caliphal institutions and city institutions. They both occupied buildings within the city, and the relationships between those institutions does not seem to have had much influence on the shape of the city. For example, when al-Mansur left the round city to reside in Qasr al-Khuld, few institutions relocated with him, and those that did were mainly caliphal ones. City institutions continued, at least for a while, to occupy the center of the round city.[61]

During its early years Baghdad possessed only one Friday mosque and one *qadi*, or judge. The *qadi* initially held court in the mosque. Although, as we have seen, other Friday mosques were being established in different parts of the city, the position of *qadi* continued to be held by one individual only until the later part of the ninth century.[62]

Before the end of his reign, al-Mansur had come to see that the Baghdad, which he envisioned as the small circular city called Madinat al-Salam, developed

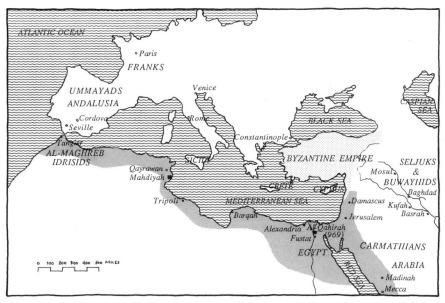

FIGURE 5.10 The North African Movement and the Rise of the Fatimids.

a life of its own and had become its own organism. But again it was not only Baghdad that was changing; the caliphate was changing too. Now the caliphs had established themselves as supreme rulers who were not willing to accept any challenge to their authority to govern as they considered it their inherent God-given right. This had a negative impact on the Abbasid Empire, and by the end of the tenth century A.D. much of the empire was divided among rising dynasties of governors and amirs who claimed independence from Baghdad. The real threat, however, to the legitimacy of the Abbasid caliphate was still broiling in the lands of North Africa.

THE RISE OF THE FATIMIDS AND THE PLANNING OF CAIRO

Egypt and North Africa were among the first states to gain some sort of autonomy in the far-flung and loosely controlled Abbasid empire. In Tunisia, the movement against the decadent Abbasid caliphs reached its peak when Sa'id ibn Husain al-Mahdi, an alleged descendent of the Alids, broke away from the empire and established the Shiite Fatimid caliphate[63] (**FIGURE 5.10**).

The Fatimids were intent on moving eastward, possibly to challenge the Abbasids. After successive attempts, their movement gathered enough momentum to permit the conquest of Egypt. Al-Mu'izz, who was the fourth Fatimid caliph, appointed Jawhar al-Siqeli to lead his forces in the Egyptian campaign. Jawhar, whose name literally meant "The Sicilian Jewel" in Arabic, was of Christian slave origin.[64] At the time, Egypt was ruled by the Ikhshidis, another feudalistic princedom with provincial autonomy. In 358/969, the Fatimids easily defeated the Ikhshidis and marched through the cities of Fustat and Al-Qata'ia, the latter being the capital of the Ikhshidis[65] (FIGURE 5.11).

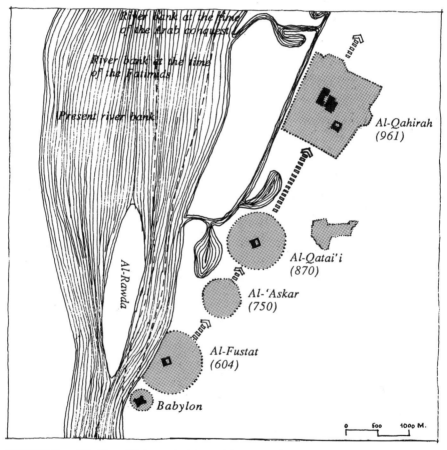

FIGURE 5.11 The Site of Cairo at the Time of the Fatimid Invasion and the Relationship of the New Capital al-Qahirah to the Older Cities that Superceded It.

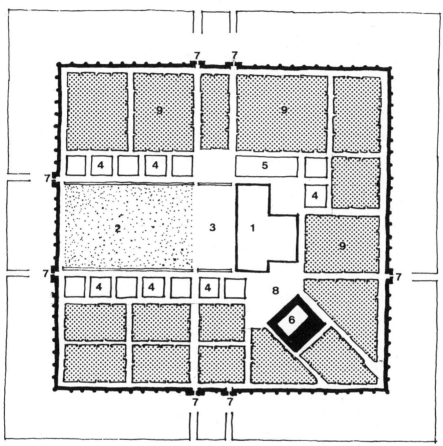

1. Caliphal 2. Garden 3. Maidan 4. Royal Palaces 5. Guest House 6. Mosque 7. Gates 8. Rahbah 9. Residential Quarters

FIGURE 5.12 The Original Plan of al-Qahirah, Initially Envisioned by Jawhar as al-Mansuriyah (A Reconstruction Based on al-Maqrizi's Description of the Plan).

Almost immediately after his arrival, Jawhar began to search for a site to garrison his troops. According to at least one account, he carried with him some ideas about the construction of a new capital, which al-Mu'izz envisioned as the seat of his caliphate and as a rival to Baghdad.[66]

As Jawhar had to impose on this fragmented region his predetermined plan, he located the new city in the only site available to him to the north of the existing settlements.[67] Seen in context, al-Qaherah was another addition to an existing pattern of cities that paralleled the Nile. This pattern started in 640 A.D. when Amr Ibn al-'As built his mosque close to the remains of an ancient fortress and established to its north the garrison town of Fustat. Later, with the first dynastic shift, the Abbasids built the town of al-'Askar in 750 A.D. to the north of Fustat to house their troops. When in 870 A.D. Ahmad ibn Tulun declared Egypt's independence from the Abbasid caliphate, he founded al-Qata'ia as his own princely city and again this was to the north of al-'Askar. Jawhar's choice of al-Qaherah's site conformed with this north-south urban axis that tied the new city to its predecessors (Refer to FIGURE 5.11).

Jawhar's first step was to lay down the city wall, determine the gates, and start construction of the two major buildings: the caliphal palace and the mosque.[68] Legend has it that on the following day, when a delegation from Fustat went to welcome Jawhar, they found that foundation for the entire city had already been dug.[69] The chronicles contain no mention of architects or builders involved in this process, leading us to the belief that his army may have included individuals with such specialized skills.

Al-Maqrizi, the renowned historian of Cairo, relates that Jawhar initially planned the city as a square with sides equaling 1,200 yards each. This defined a total area of 340 acres, of which 70 acres were alloted to the caliphal palace, 70 other acres to the existing gardens, *al-Bustan al-Kafuri*, and new squares or *rahbahs*. The remaining acreage was assigned as *khutat* to the twenty different groups making up the army[70] (FIGURE 5.12).

As in Baghdad, Jawhar consulted with his astrologers before deciding on the location of the town or the date of executing his plan. In fact, several sources relate that the town was later called "al-Qaherah" after a bright star the astrologer observed in the sky that night.[71]

Al-Maqrizi also reports that Jawhar started laying out the town on the evening of a Friday in the month of Sha'aban in 358/969. Since he was so anxious to implement his plans, he ordered his soldiers to carry on throughout the night, and in the morning he realized that the plan had been implemented with

---

1. Big Eastern Palace 2. Small Western Palace 3. Palace Square 4. Al-Azhar Mosque 5. Guest House 6. Minister's House 7. Stables 8. Kafuri Garden 9. Al-Hakim Mosque 10. Mosque 11. Gates 12. Residential Quarters: A. *Farahiyah* B. *Bergoan* C. *'Outoufiyah* D. *Barqiyah* E. *Koutamah* F. *Tawareq* G. *Sharabiyah* H. *Greek* I. *Daiylam* J. *'Umarah* K. *Judariyah* L. *Zuaiylah* M. *Mahmudiyah* N. *'Uzriyah*

FIGURE 5.13 (FACING PAGE) A Reconstruction of the Plan of al-Qahirah as Implemented on Site, Based on the Egyptian Geographic Society Map of 1922.

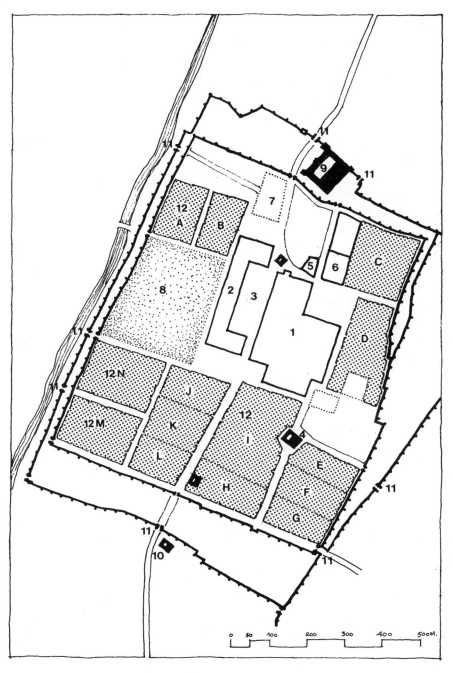

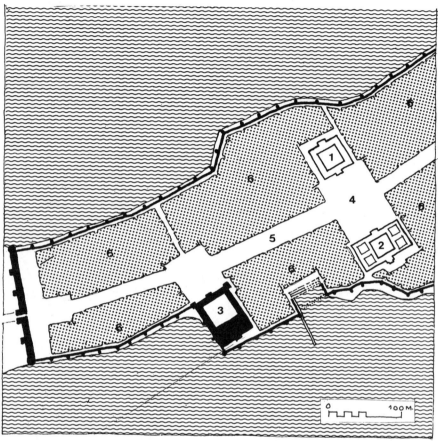

1. *Abul Qasem's Palace* 2. *'Ubaiydallah's Palace* 3. *Great Mosque* 4. *Square* 5. *Main Thoroughfare* 6. *Residential Quarters*

FIGURE 5.14 The Plan of Al-Mahdiyah Reconstructed.

inconsistencies that had resulted in a slightly distorted rectangular shape. He then decided not to correct it, saying that "it was laid out in a holy night and that its irregularity must have been caused by a divine logic"[72] (**FIGURE 5.13**).

It is unlikely that during execution the plan could have been so severely distorted from its original square shape into a rectangle as some scholars believe. The sides of the executed plan carry the proportion of 2:3, a proportion not likely to be achieved as a result of a mistake. The original plan has also been the subject of continual controversy. Marcel Clerget believes that Caliph al-Muʿizz designed the city himself and provided Jawhar with a precise plan with specific dimensions and a proposed procedure for execution.[73] C. J. Haswell had earlier suggested that the plan of Cairo was initially envisioned along the lines of a Roman *castrum*.[74] Other scholars, however, maintained that the plan was simply intended as a duplicate of the Fatimid towns of al-Mahdiyah or al-Mansuriyah in Tunis.[75] I cannot substantiate these propositions since the executed plan of Cairo appears, at least visually, quite distinct if compared to al-Mahdiyah (FIGURE 5.14).

Whether it was modeled after a Roman *castrum* or a North African town, Jawhar started the construction of the city by building a palace, a mosque, and a mud brick wall around them. He called the city al-Mansuriyah after a city built by al-Mu'izz's father in Tunisia. Most of the gates of the new city were named after the gates of al-Mansuriyah in Tunis, providing additional support to the view that the city was modeled after its North African counterpart.[76]

Four years after the conquest, Caliph al-Mu'izz arrived at the new city and declared it the capital of his caliphate. The caliph then changed its name to al-Qaherah, meaning "the Victorious."[77] The name was later distorted by Italian travelers to its current English name: Cairo.[78]

Caliph al-Mu'izz was from the beginning intent on creating an imperial capital with an instant sense of history. He brought with him from Tunis three coffins enclosing the remains of his predecessors and ordered their burial in a site close to his palace. As he arrived in the city, the caliph led the first public prayer, setting Cairo on the tracks of being the religious and intellectual capital of the Muslim world for years to come.[79] The Abbasid caliph's name was eliminated from all official records and prayers, and new coinage was struck. In place of black, the offical color of the Abbasids, white was ordained. For the first time in a thousand years Egypt became a sovereign state headed by one person: the Fatimid caliph who was both a spiritual and a political leader.[80]

ORIGINAL ELEMENTS OF FATIMID CAIRO

Al-Maqrizi's description of the different urban elements that make up the Fatimid city exceeds a couple of hundred pages, of which a considerable portion is devoted to its palaces. He reports that Jawhar and his forces camped to the south of the site of al-Qaherah and that they immediately started building the city walls. Al-Maqrizi also relates that Jawhar started concurrently the construction of the main palace in 358/969.[81] The palace apparently included several

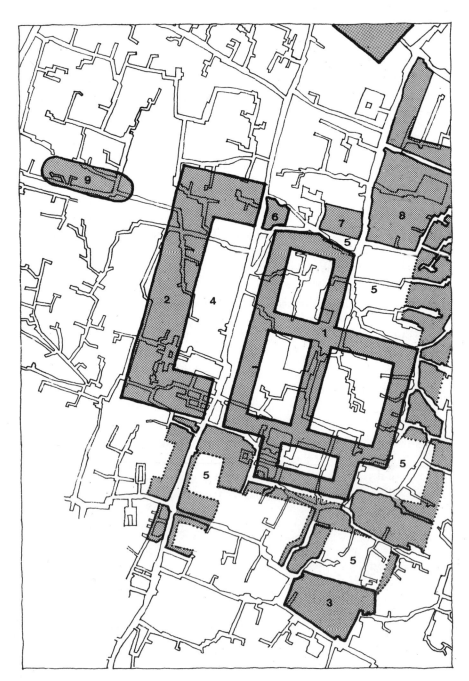

large halls and opened out to the rest of the city through nine gates. One scholar attempted a reconstruction of this palace which occupied the center of the city (FIGURE 5.15).

The palace bordered from its western side the central square, or the *maidan*, later circumscribed by the addition of another caliphal palace further west. Mubarak relates that the *maidan* acted as a place where the caliph would review his troops, and it was a huge space that accommodated 10,000 soldiers.[82] Again, like Baghdad, the caliphal palace was isolated from all its surroundings by a few spaces, squares, and gardens. To its west was al-Bustan al-Kafuri, a large garden established as a retreat during the time of the Ikhsheeds. The garden was walled and connected by underground tunnels to the caliphal palace. It was exclusively reserved in the early days for use by the caliph and his family.[83] From the north and the east *rahbahs* separated the caliphal palace from the guest house and the *khutah* of al-Barqiya respectively.

Although the spatial configuration around the caliphal palace seems irregular, it nevertheless emulated the concept of isolating the caliph from his subjects and placing him at the center of the settlement, a precedent set in place by the first planned Islamic capital, Baghdad (FIGURE 5.16).

While the construction of the palace was going on, Jawhar decided to embark on the building of a Friday mosque to the south of the palace and separated from it mainly by a *rahbah*. Al-Maqrizi relates that construction of the mosque started in 359/970 and that it was completed three years later. Caliph Al-Mu'izz led the first Friday prayer and delivered the *khutbah* sermon on the first Friday of Ramadan in 361/972 in al-Azhar.[84] It is very difficult to know the origin of the plan of the mosque for it was subjected to several changes over the years. Throughout its early years, however, the al-Azhar served as the only congregational mosque in the city, and it was not until the reign of Caliph al-'Aziz that it became a major institute of Islamic learning.[85]

Like Baghdad, the *haras*, or residential quarters of al-Qaherah, occupied the outer circumference of the city, although at a very different proportion. There were originally twenty *haras*, and one assigned to each of the tribes making up

---

▨ *Area of Palaces   1. Eastern Palace 2. Western Palace 3. Al-Azhar Mosque 4. Palace Square (occupied later by Ayyubid and Mamluke buildings) 5. Square (Maiydan) 6. Al-Aqmar Mosque 7. Guest House 8. Palace of the Wazir 9. Stables & Horse Riding*

FIGURE 5.15 (FACING PAGE) Ravaisse's Reconstruction of the Fatimid Palatial Quarters in the Center of al-Qahirah.

the Fatimid army. The balance achieved between those tribes, and their representation in the government of Fatimid Cairo, was of major importance to its urban existence. Unlike the early garrison towns, which were mostly populated by tribes from Arabia, al-Qaherah was not composed of a homogeneous group. Urban order existed by virtue of a system that allowed all the different groups a share in urban government.[86]

As a private princely town, the original city does not seem to have contained any major markets. None of the chronicles gives any mention to such an activity. It is very possible, though, that during its early days the city contained warehouses and small neighborhood markets for the residents of the different quarters; it would have otherwise been very inconvenient for those residents to have to go out of the city for their immediate shopping needs. As we will see later, this situation changed as the city grew larger and as it developed a balanced relationship with its twin city, Fustat.

So the image of the city of al-Muʿizz seems to be one that conforms to a regular grid with wide streets and large open squares, very much different from the stereotypical image of the Muslim city (FIGURES 5.17 and 5.18).

FIGURE 5.16 (ABOVE AND FACING PAGE) Two Views Representing a Reconstruction of Early Fatimid al-Qahirah.

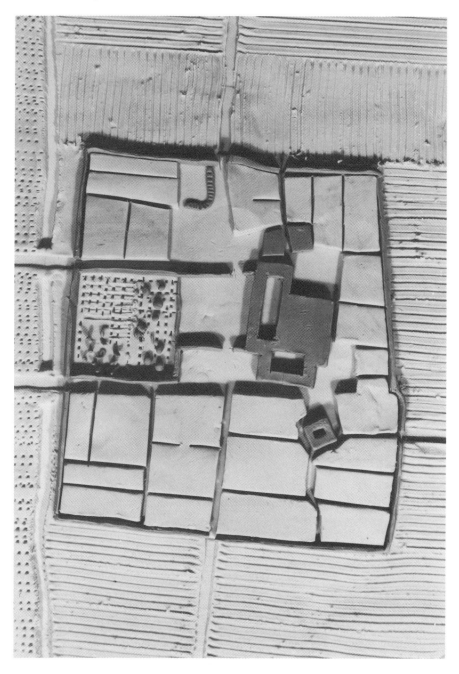

THE CHANGING PATTERN OF THE FATIMID CITY

Although it was al-Mu'izz's vision that brought al-Qaherah to existence, he did not live long enough to enjoy his new capital. When al-Mu'izz died in 365/975, his son al-'Aziz took over the caliphate and was destined to reign a little more than twenty years. Al-'Aziz was a great builder, and during his reign several important buildings were added to al-Qaherah. Among these were the western Palace and the al-Anwar Mosque.

The small western palace, also known as Qasr al-Bahr, was of great urban significance to the city. Initially built as a residence for one of his daughters, the palace defined the central *maidan* of al-Qaherah and separated it from the caliphal gardens (Refer to FIGURE 5.15). When al-Mustansir ascended to the caliphate in 427/1036 at a time corresponding to the downfall of the Abassid caliphate, he refurbished the palace in preparation for making it the official residence of the deposed Abassid caliph. This represented al-Mustansir's attempt to bestow more legitimacy on his own caliphate by adopting the relocated caliphate of the Abbasids.[87]

The Anwar mosque, which later became known as the mosque of al-Hakim, was initiated during the rule of al-Aziz to act as a new *khutbah* mosque to accommodate the Friday and feast prayers. Al-Maqrizi mentions that al-'Aziz prayed in this mosque before its construction was completed. When he died, his son al-Hakim finished the building.[88] The urban significance of the mosque of al-Hakim, built outside the Bab al-Futuh gate, lies in the fact that it was the first Fatimid mosque ever built outside the walls of the Fatimid city. Its construction, which utilized dismantled building materials of an ancient Egyptian building, also signaled a change in the pattern of religious preaching in Cairo. For the first time, the Friday *khutbah* was held in more than one mosque. The mosque of Amr in the city of Fustat, accommodated the Sunni *Khutbah*, while the Shiite *Khutbah* was held in the mosque of al-Hakim and the mosque of al-Azhar, which now served primarily as an institute for Islamic studies.[89]

Another important building added to al-Qaherah during the reign of al-Hakim was the Dar al-Hikmah, or the house of wisdom. This building was

---

1. Caliphal Palace 2. Al-Azhar Mosque 3. Palatial Gardens (Al-Bustan al-Kafuri) 4. Guest House (Dar al-Diafah) 5. Stables 6.Squares: A. *Caliphal Square (Al-Maiydan al-Kabir)* B. *Maiydan al-'Ikhshid* C. *Rahbah al-Qasr* D. *Rahbah al-Azhar* E. *Rahbah Qasr al-Shouk* F. *Rahbah al-'Id* G. *Rahbah Dar al-Diafah*

FIGURE 5.17 (FACING PAGE) A Reconstruction of Early al-Qahirah, Showing the Caliphal Palace Isolated from Its Surroundings by Open Spaces, Based on al-Maqrizi.

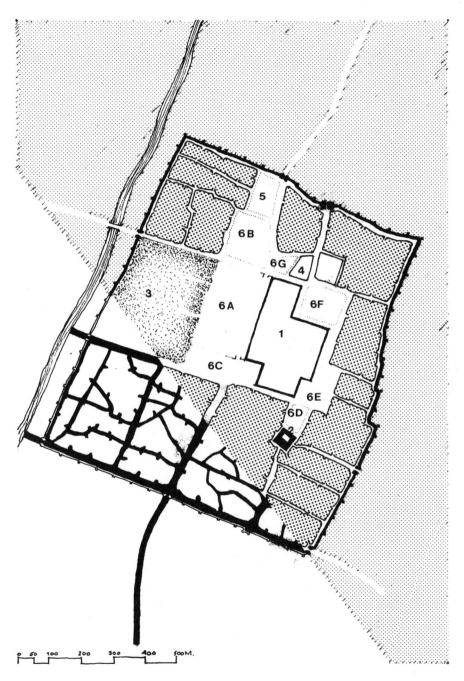

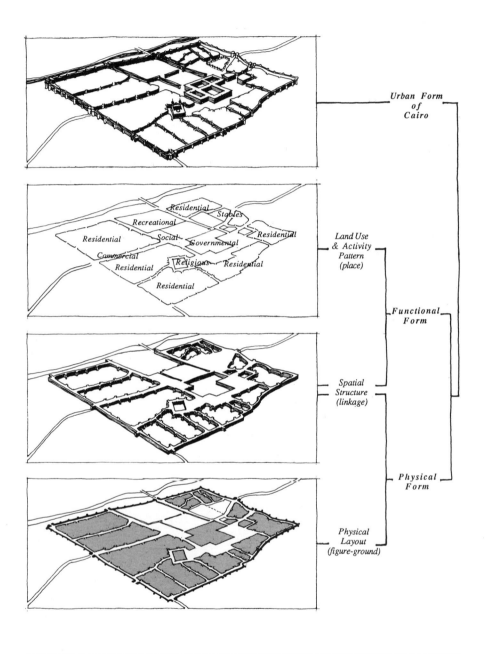

FIGURE 5.18 The Urban Form of Fatimid Cairo Analyzed.

constructed to the north of the western palace and acted as a center for scientific and literary scholars.[90]

In 462/1068, Egypt suffered a severe drought, and with the spread of the plague, urban order in Cairo disintegrated. The situation in Cairo degenerated to the extent that the caliph of the time, al-Mustansir, had to call on his governor in Syria, Badr al-Jamali, to take over the government of Egypt. Badr was a very strong ruler who managed to restore order to the capital and revive the political and religious authority of the Fatimid caliphate.[91]

Badr also renewed the appearance of the city. His achievements included enlarging the city by building a new stone wall and a series of new gates so as to include all of the buildings that were built outside the wall. For the first time, al-Qaherah was given the appearance of a fortified city, an accomplishment that was primarily achieved by using recycled stone from nearby ancient Egyptian temples and by importing skilled builders of defensive structures from Byzantium. Badr also built the Dar al-Wizarah, or the residence of the *wazir*, to the northeast side of the central palace. This building acted as the official residence of all Fatimid *wazirs* until the fall of the Fatimid caliphate.[92]

Fatimid al-Qaherah was an impressive city in its heyday. Although from the beginning it was only envisioned as a large palatial compound, it quickly developed into a full urban center. The Persian traveler Nasiri Khusraw, who resided in the city from 441/1047 to 444/1050, gives a brief description of the extent of trade and commerce inside a city that was not designed to have any shops at its inception in 361/969. Khusraw mentions that the number of shops inside the city exceeded 20,000, accommodating all types of commercial activity. All of the shops were owned by the caliph and were rented. Most of the shop tenants resided in Fustat and commuted to their shops. No one was allowed to own commercial or residential property in al-Qaherah except the caliph.[93]

Before the end of Fatimid rule, the two cities — al-Qaherah and al-Fustat — existed side by side and acted as one urban center that served as the true capital of the Fatimid caliphate and the most important city of medieval Islam. Later, when the Ayyubids took over the city, they opened it up to the commoners who lived outside its walls. The regular pattern of the planned city started to disintegrate and look more like its older neighbor, Fustat[94] (FIGURE 5.19).

THE FORM OF THE PLANNED CAPITAL TOWN

Are Cairo and Baghdad similar in any way? Do they share any common characteristics? Is their form a representation of Islamic urban ideals? And do

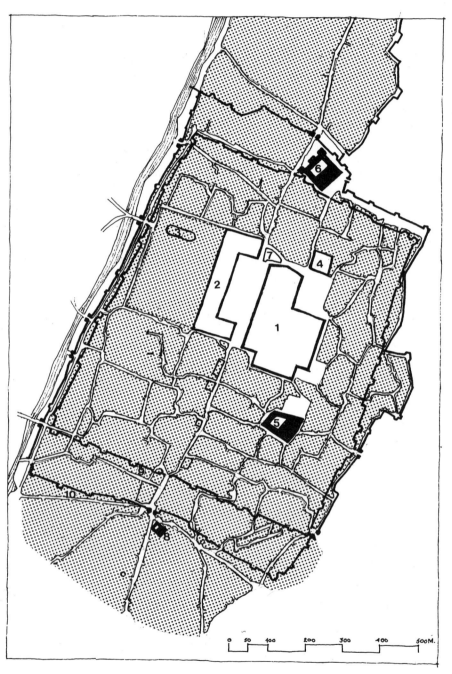

their forms reveal anything about the Islamic system? In terms of compositional elements, location of activities, process of building, and general symbolism, Cairo and Baghdad seem to share many commonalities.

Since they were both established as new capital cities for new dynasties, Cairo and Baghdad started as large palatial compounds containing a palace, a Friday mosque, a central square, and residential quarters for the tribal troops that composed the army. From the little we know, they had this much in common with the stereotypical Muslim city. But, unlike the stereotypical city, Cairo and Baghdad in their early days had no public baths, specialized markets, or citadels. They also had no irregular dead-end streets, and their spatial structure conformed to a very geometric pattern. Of course, later developments changed all that.

In terms of the location of activities, the caliphal palace, which also acted as a governmental complex, occupied the physical center of both Cairo and Baghdad. The mosque was either a side building attached to the palace, as in the case of Baghdad, or simply a building that occupied a nearby site, as in the case of Cairo. As a building, the Friday mosque was certainly a secondary one in terms of its proximity to the center and its visual importance, if compared to the palace. Residential quarters occupied the outer circumference of the two cities.

The process of building Cairo and Baghdad was also similar. First a palace was built, then a wall circumscribing the city was constructed. During the same time a mosque was added to accommodate Friday prayers. This situation was different from that of the early *amsar* where the mosque was always the first element to be built because of the functional need for it and because it represented the authority of the new state. In capital towns, the caliphal palace substituted for the mosque in its role as a symbolic representation of a new dynasty. The Islamic religion was already two hundred years old and enjoyed a substantial number of followers, and the new caliphs felt a greater need to establish their own dynastic authority than they did to continue the Islamic symbolic appropriation of the land.

But before construction of the new capital was finished, changes started immediately to take place. First there was an enlargement of the palace or the

1. Caliphal Eastern Palace 2. Western Palace 3. Stables 4. Wazir's Palace 5. Al-Azhar Mosque 6. Al-Hakim Mosque 7. Al-Aqmar Mosque 8. Al-Saleh Mosque 9. Old Walls & Gates 10. New Walls & Gates

FIGURE 5.19 (FACING PAGE) Al-Qahirah at the End of the Fatimid Rule, After Ravaisse.

building of a new palace, either outside of the city, as in the case of al-Khuld palace in Baghdad, or inside it, as in the case of the western palace in Cairo. This movement signified the caliph's desire to isolate himself even further from the population.

The market element was also subject to changes. In Baghdad the markets were first moved from the individual neighborhoods and placed in the arcaded colonnades of the residential quarters. Later, they were completely relocated outside in Karakh so as to free the city for the caliph and ensure his safety. In Cairo, markets were not initially designed as part of al-Qaherah proper. When they were later added, another device to regulate them and to control the power of the merchant class was implemented. The merchants were not allowed to own their shops but had to rent them from the caliph; no one had the right to own any property in the city but the caliph. By preventing them also from residing inside the gated city, where their source of livelihood existed, the caliph could ensure their obedience and instill a sense of uncertainty in their lives.

The typical elements and general arrangement of a planned capital city do not appear very different from other Muslim towns discussed earlier. But Cairo and Baghdad are not necessarily good representative examples of Muslim cities. These two cities, frequently used by urban and architectural historians as typical Muslim cities, were unique in that, for quite a while, they simply acted as refuge within which the new alien caliph and his entourage could separate themselves from the rest of the local population and live an isolated royal life. And this was achieved at great expense and with great deliberation.

To go back to some of the questions posed at the beginning of this chapter, it is important to remember that Cairo and Baghdad came into existence as a result of the prior conceptions and individual will of their creators, the caliphs. If Islam is defined as a comprehensive cultural system based on a religious principle, then the physical forms of these cities were not representative of any Islamic building or planning ideals. This is particularly true if we reject the alleged divine authority claimed by some caliphs. Cities planned by caliphs for themselves instead of for their people should not be considered a proper representation of Islam as a religious or cultural system. In this sense, the symbolism in the physical form of Cairo or Baghdad is not Islamic and possibly not Arabic.

It is also important for us here to note the similarities between the early garrison towns like Kufah and Basrah and the planned capitals like Cairo and Baghdad, especially in terms of their physical elements and the general arrangement of those elements on site. Garrison towns, in spite of their pure symbolic qualities, may have been prototypes for later princely capital towns such as Cairo and Baghdad.

In the case of the later group, the location of the major elements and their relationship to each other was more representative of the power of the caliph and the authority of the state than in the garrison towns. This could be observed in the centrality of the palace, the decreasing importance of the mosque as a building, the constant disregard for the stability of the market place, and the desire to limit the general public's access to the city.

Planned capital towns, like Cairo and Baghdad, were physical expressions of symbolic power. Their names either glorified their founders and their ancestors or perpetuated a specific concept of politico-religious authority. Their physical elements were directly symbolic of the institutional structure of an Islamic capital city. The relationship of those elements to each other was iconographic because it was an indirect representation of the hidden order that governed early Muslim urban societies.

VI

EPILOGUE

THE ARAB MUSLIM CITY AND THE GENESIS OF URBAN FORM: RELIGIOUS IDEOLOGY VERSUS CALIPHAL AUTHORITY

This work was originally about the building of Arab Muslim cities. It was not meant to be a comprehensive survey of their forms or of the literature on their development, but rather simply an attempt to go back to the original sources to shed a new light on the origins of Muslim urbanism. As we have seen, it has been very difficult to characterize the cities included in this work as Islamic or Muslim, mainly because they were created out of a variety of forces and circumstances, of which Islam was only one. The use of the adjective "Muslim" to describe their physical forms is only justified when it is further modified by the adjectives "early" and "Arab."

The Arab chroniclers, who provided the major sources of this study, wrote mainly about the history of the Muslim caliphs and their personalities, and it is only through this history that we were able to write about the historical development of Islamic places. The story of the building of the Arab Muslim city will remain incomplete until a history of common Muslim persons is written.

In the early days of Islam, the Arabs, who showed some resistance to assimilation, built towns that bore a striking similarity to the city of Madinah, the first Arab Muslim city. These were garrison towns like Basrah and Kufah whose physical form emerged from a process of arbitration. The internal organization of each such town was negotiated between the governor of the town and its inhabitants, while its overall form resulted from negotiations between the caliph, who was concerned with enforcing the Islamic ideal of community, and the governor, who had to deal with the immediate needs of the local population. The early form of the garrison town represented some Islamic principles modified by Arab nomadic experiences and ideals. As each garrison town grew older, its form began to be determined more by the individual will of its governor than by any other Islamic religious principle or administrative rationale.

At the same time that garrison towns were being built, the Arabs were taking over existing well-established towns. The transformation of these towns that preexisted Islamic rule seems to have followed a consistent pattern that was part of an unselfconscious program put in place by the caliphs and amirs to bring about the Islamization of the city fabric. The changes that ensued were not, however, representative of any Islamic ideology but were rather a reflection of the ever-changing nature of the Arab people. The changes in the form of existing cities, like Damascus and Cordova, reflected the realization on the part of the Arab caliphs that survival of their new empire necessitated the encouragement of un-Islamic practices, such as monument-building.

Capital towns, like Cairo and Baghdad, came into existence as a result of elaborate acts of single individuals. Their urban forms were not representative of any Islamic or Arabic planning ideals, if such things ever existed. As capitals, they were physical expressions of symbolic power, and their city forms perpetuated the concept of politico-religious authority embodied in the system of the caliphate.

It has become fashionable to speak of the irregularity of forms in Arab Muslim cities as a response to social and legal codes and as a representation of the Islamic cultural system. Although this remains true for many cities in the Middle East, this study has shown that planned Arab Muslim towns were originally designed according to very regular geometric patterns. That they achieved an irregular form in later years was probably due to many factors whose scope has not been covered here.

Generally speaking, the stereotypical Muslim city with its central palace, mosque, residential quarters, and bazaars is not a total fiction. All Arab Muslim cities have contained, at one point or another, elements of this stereotype. The central mosque is the most common of these. As we have seen, all towns, regardless of their type, had one and only one mosque in their early stages, which the caliphs and amirs tried to maintain as the only place for public prayers at the expense of tribal neighborhood *masjids*. Later, as the political, administrative, and population structure changed, caliphs and amirs found it to their advantage to establish other mosques, and this seems to have changed forever the visual and functional importance of the central mosque.

In the early days the importance of the mosque was also represented in the fact that it was the first building to be laid out or designated in either a new town or an existing town. In later decades, the palace of the caliph or the amir replaced it in terms of centrality of location. The central place of both Cairo and Baghdad was laid out first and was located at the center of the settlement. The mosque was later attached to it or built in a close-by location. This reflected the changing importance of the mosque and possibly the entire role of religion, now being replaced by the authority of the Caliph.

In early Basrah, Kufah, Damascus, and even Baghdad, the mosque and the palace existed as a single integral building in the center of the town. Their centrality symbolized the unity of politics and religion in a new rising Islamic empire. The nature of the caliphate and the emirate as the leadership of the Muslims in all activities sacred and secular was expressed architecturally by the proximity of the *Masjid* to *Dar al-Imarah* or *Dar al-Khilafat*, although as we have seen this relationship was considered by some an accidental one. When this politico-religious complex was split into two separate, distant buildings, the functions of state and religion in the Muslim city were separated for many years to come.

The changing nature of the relationship between the mosque and the palace is very clearly demonstrated in a comparison of Basrah and Cairo. In Basrah, the mosque was placed at the center and the Dar al-Imarah was attached to it. Three centuries later and some hundred miles to the west, this central place was reserved for the caliphal palace of Cairo while the mosque was pushed away to the side. This signified the rise of caliphal authority and the decline of religious ideology as fundamental shapers of the form of the Muslim city.

In general, the early Arabs remained without any architectural ambitions, and when they began to feel such a need, it was chiefly for political reasons, because most of the time the Arabs had to turn to the advanced architectural talents of the conquered peoples to achieve their urban intentions. Their acceptance and later adoption of building as a mode of enforcing their rule reflected a growing authoritarian control of their rulers.

When the Arabs recognized the importance of building, everything became legitimate as a means to build an architectural image representative of their cultural development. Dismantling buildings or ruins of earlier civilizations to build their new cities and mosques became a common Islamic building pattern. We have seen it in the construction of the garrison town of Kufah and the round capital city of al-Mansur in Baghdad, where some of the building materials were borrowed from earlier Sassanian palaces in Ctesiphon and other Persian cities.

We saw it again in the construction of Ummayad palaces in Damascus, the walls of Cairo, and the mosque of al-Hakim where the stones were taken from nearby ancient Byzantine churches and Egyptian temples respectively.

Appropriating the religious buildings of earlier civilizations was also a common practice of the early Arabs. We saw it in Damascus, Aleppo, and Cordova, where temples and churches were taken over and transformed into mosques. Although this practice was in itself un-Islamic, the early Arabs seem to have found it legitimate. They came to accept it because it was relatively easy and because it allowed them to capitalize on the central location of such buildings within the city.

One can observe a certain continuity in the urban forms of Arab-Muslim cities. This continuity was evident in the desire to preserve the symbolism that developed in the early days, even though it may not have represented any Islamic ideals. Examples of that included naming new cities and palaces after earlier places, as in the cases of palaces built outside a city. In Damascus, when the caliph moved out of the city, he called his new palace al-Rusafah. The name was later given by caliphs of later dynasties to palaces outside Baghdad and Cordova. In Egypt, the Fatimids initially named their city al-Mansuriyah, after an earlier one in Tunis. This reuse of the name in a similar move signified their desire to continue the same earlier symbolism or the same earlier relationship established by their predecessors or competing rivals.

We see this again in the reuse of the green dome in the caliphal palaces. The Ummayads were the first to use a green dome in the palace of Mu'awiyah, which neighbored the Damascus mosque. Green was the color of the Ummayad flag, and its use in the dome was probably an extension of Ummayad identity. Because the Ummayads were the first dynastic caliphs, the color became associated with the authority of the caliphate. Later, when the Abbasids took over, they changed the flag color to black. But when al-Mansur was building his palace in the round city of Baghdad, he chose to use green again, as we have seen, as a color for its dome. Al-Mansur was legitimizing his caliphate and his palace as its physical representation by choosing a color that was used earlier in Damascus by the first dynastic caliph in the first Dar al-Khilafat. The green dome had now come to be a symbol of Islamic imperial authority.

Continuity in the form of the Arab Muslim city can also be observed in the continuous influence of non-Muslim visitors in decisions that shaped its form. Earlier we have seen three cases in which opinion and sayings by Byzantine ambassadors seem to have had a major impact on an ensuing change in the form of Arab Muslim cities. In Damascus, Mu'awiyah, the first Ummayad caliph, decided to rebuild his house after it was reported that the Byzantine ambassador shunned it as poor. In later years, the Ummayad caliph, 'Umar II, abandoned his plans to dismantle the lavish decorations of the Damascus mosque after he was told that the Byzantine delegation that visited it was very impressed by it. A hundred years later, the Abbasid caliph al-Mansur decided to move the markets outside the round city when the Byzantine ambassador brought to his attention the danger they posed to his security and personal safety.

Although the authenticity of those reports that describe how the caliphs were influenced by the opinions of foreign ambassadors may be questionable, the Arab historians who reported them must have been aware that attributing many of those caliphal decisions to outside foreign influence would have made their caliphs look weak. Although this may be partially true, one should not deny that there were always functional and symbolic reasons behind those decisions. In the case of the Ummayad caliphs, Mu'awiyah's concern for establishing himself as the king of the Arabs was behind many of his actions. 'Umar II was motivated by his desires to maintain what he perceived as pure Islam. His acceptance of the symbolic role of lavish monumental buildings was only an extension of his attitudes. The Abbasid caliph al-Mansur was, on the other hand, motivated by his concern for his own personal safety, and he took steps to remedy an existing safety problem. What the Byzantine ambassadors said was only significant because it prompted the caliphs to take a necessary action to build an urban image for the new religion. In an odd way the early caliphs, possibly seduced by Western ideas, were the real planners of Arab Muslim cities.

As we already know, Muslim cities existed by virtue of the interaction between a number of different groups that made Muslim urban society. This is more true in the case of the early Arab Muslim city than for any later date, and the form of the Arab Muslim city was also a reflection of this structure. At the time the garrison towns were founded, the institutions of Islam were not fully developed and the form of such towns was more a representation of a process of arbitration and power sharing than any established Islamic institutional structure. The transformed towns witnessed the development and modification of existing urban institutions. The form of those transformed towns represented the institutional fragmentation of Muslim urban society. But by the time the capital cities were being established, the urban institution of Islam had fully matured. The form of the capital town was representative of caliphal power and institutional authority.

The Arabs' changing perception of the role of buildings and their recognition of the importance of architecture was to some extent behind the changing urban form of the Arab Muslim city. In some sense, the early cities of Islam, built or occupied by the Arabs, were initiated as Islamic, became increasingly Arabized, and were finally molded by regional contexts and local political circumstances. It is appropriate to conclude that the change in the form of the Arab Muslim city was a reflection of the changing nature of a particular group of the human race and of their emergence as new people on an old land in an ever-changing world.

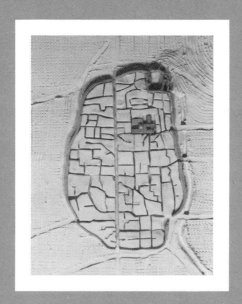

NOTES

CHAPTER I

1. A. A. Duri, *The Rise of Historical Writing among the Arabs,* Lawrence Conrad, trans. (Princeton: Princeton University Press, 1983).
2. Nezar AlSayyad, "Notes on the Muslim City: Physical Aspects," in J. Wineman, R. Barnes, and C. Zimrig, eds., *The Cost of Not Knowing: Proceedings of the 1986 EDRA Conference* (Madison, Wisc.: Omnipress, 1986), pp. 15–22. For a detailed discussion on different opinions regarding the diversity of Islamic Architecture and urban form, refer to the Dogan Kuban-Oleg Grabar debates on this issue in the *Seminar Proceedings of the Aga Khan Award for Architecture,* 1–5 (1978–1982). Also Dogan Kuban, "The Geographical and Historical Bases of the Diversity of Muslim Architectural Styles," in A. Germen, ed., *Islamic Architecture and Urbanism* (Dammam: King Faisal University Press, 1963), pp. 1–6, and Oleg Grabar, "The Iconography of Islamic Architecture," in A. Germen, ed., *Ibid.,* pp. 6–17.
3. J. Wagstaff, "The Origin and Evolution of Towns," in G. Blake and R. Lawless, eds., *The Changing Middle Eastern City* (London: Crown Helm, 1983), p. 20.
4. Protagonists of this argument include: William Marcais, "L'Islamisme et la vie urbanie," in *Articles and Conferences* (Paris, 1961), pp. 59–67; George Marcais, "La Conception des villes dans L'Islam," in *Revue d'Alger* (Algiers, 1955), pp. 517–533; Jean Sauvaget, *Alep* (Paris, Librairie Orientaliste, 1941), and "Le plan de Laodicee-Sur-Mer," in *Bulletin d'Etude Orientals* (Paris, 1934), vol. 4; P. Deffontaines, *Geographie et Religion* (Paris, 1948), p. 147; Gustave Von Grunebaum, *Islam: Essays in the Nature and Growth of a Cultural Tradition* (London: Routledge and Kegan Paul, 1955); and Xavier De Planhol, *World of Islam* (Ithaca: Cornell University Press, 1959).
5. Protagonists of this argument include: F. Benet, "The Ideology of Islamic Urbanization," in N. Anderson, ed., *Urbanization and Urbanism* (London: E. J. Brill, 1964); and E. Pauty, "Villes spontanees et villes crees en Islam," in *Annales de L'Institute d'Etude Orientals 9* (1950).

6. Protagonists of this argument include: William Fischel, "The City in Islam," in *Middle Eastern Affairs 7* (1956); and Roger LeTourneau, *Les Villes Musulmanes des L'Afrique du Nord* (Algiers, 1957).

7. Ira Lapidus, "Evolution of Early Muslim Urban Society," in *Comparative Studies in Society and History 15* (1973), pp. 21–50.

8. Robert Adams, *Land Behind Baghdad* (Chicago: University of Chicago Press, 1965).

9. Gamal Hamdan, "The Pattern of Medieval Urbanism in the Arab World," in *Geography 47* (1962), pp. 121–134; and Roger LeTourneau, *op. cit.*

10. Ira Lapidus, *op. cit.*, 1973; and Gamal Hamdan, *op. cit.*, 1962.

11. Paul Claval, "Reflections on the Cultural Geography of the European City," in J. Agnew, J. Mercer, and D. Sopher, eds., *The City in Cultural Context* (Boston: Allen and Unwin, 1984), pp. 31–49.

12. *Ibid.*, p. 37.

13. Xavier De Planhol, *op. cit.*, p. 21.

14. *Ibid.*

15. Janet Abu-Lughod, "Contemporary Relevance of Islamic Urban Principles," in A. Germen, ed., *op. cit.*, p. 64.

16. This is basically my summary of several descriptions that appear here later. It is included as a quote because, as the analysis will show, it could have come out of any of the books discussed in this chapter.

17. Kevin Lynch and Lloyd Rodwin, "The Form of the City," in Lloyd Rodwin, ed., *Cities and City Planning* (New York: Plenum Press, 1981), p. 33.

18. *Ibid.*, p. 36.

19. Roger Trancik, *Finding Lost Space* (New York: Van Nostrand Reinhold, 1986), p. 97.

20. Mostly these definitions are adapted or adopted from the work of many other scholars. I was much influenced by Harold Carter's review of urban definitions in his *Introduction to Urban Historical Geography* (London: Edward Arnold Ltd., 1983), and David Popenoe's article entitled "On the Meaning of Urban" in P. Meadows and E. Mizurchi, eds., *Urbanism, Urbanization, and Change: Comparative Perspectives* (Reading: Addison-Wesley, 1976), pp. 19–28.

21. Paul Wheatly, "The Concept of Urbanism," in Peter Ucko and Roger Tringham, eds., *Man, Settlement and Urbanism*, (London: Longman, 1967), p. 299.

22. I have adapted this definition from what appears to me to be the most convincing definition of a medieval town, that of C. T. Smith in *An Historical Geography of Western Europe* (London: Longman, 1967), p. 299.

23. L. Carl Brown, ed., *From Madina to Metropolis* (Princeton: Darwin Press, 1973), p. 24.

24. Different designations have been given to the cities of Islam by scholars from many disciplines. These will be discussed in later chapters. Ira Lapidus prefers to call such cities "Middle Eastern." Albert Hourani and R. B. Serjeant used instead the title "Islamic." Several orientalists, including Von Grunebaum and

Creswell, preferred to call them "Muslim" cities. Marshall Hodgson suggested the term "Islamicate" as a description of the higher cultural products of Islam, reserving the term "Islamic" for only those aspects that are religiously based. Most of the Arab scholars prefer instead the term "Arabic-Islamic" as a more accurate description.

CHAPTER II

1. Edward Said, *Orientalism* (New York: Vintage Books, 1979).
2. Janet Abu-Lughod, "The Islamic City — Historic Myth, Islamic Essence and Contemporary Relevance," paper presented at the annual conference of the Middle East Studies Association in 1985, later published under the same title in *International Journal of Middle East Studies 19*, 2 (May 1987).
3. William Marcais, "L'Islamisme et la Vie Urbaine," in *L'Academie des inscriptions et belles-lettres: Comptes Rendus* (Paris, 1928), pp. 86—100.
4. George Marcais, "L'Urbanisme Musulmane," in *Congres de la Federation des Societes Savantes de L'Afrique du Nord* (Algiers, 1940), pp. 31—48; and George Marcais, "La Conception des villes dans L'Islam," *Revue d'Alger* (Algiers, 1945), pp. 517—533.
5. This is my abridged translation of the description provided by George Marcais in *op. cit.*, 1940. I decided that it would be more coherent for the reader to abridge and translate this important text instead of quoting the original French text or using the more exact translation provided by Abu-Lughod in *op. cit.*, 1985.
6. Janet Abu-Lughod, *op. cit.*
7. As quoted in Abu-Lughod's translation, *op. cit.* The original text may be found in E. Renan, "Histoire Generale et Systeme de Langues Semitique," in *Oeuvres Completes* (Paris, 1840).
8. Roger LeTourneau's work includes several articles on Fez in medieval and premodern times. His books included *Les Villes Musulmanes de L'Afrique du Nord* (Algiers, 1957), *Fez in the Age of the Marinides* (Norman: University of Oklahoma Press, 1961), and *La Vie Quotidienne a Fez en 1900* (Paris, 1965).
9. Jacques Berque, "Medinas, Villesnueves et Bidonvilles," in *Les Cahiers de Tunisie* (Tunis, 1958), pp. 5—42.
10. Jean Sauvaget, "Esquisse d'une histoire de la ville de Damas," in *Revue Etudes Islamiques* (Paris, 1934) and *Alep* (Paris: Librairie Orientaliste, 1941).
11. For more on this refer to Donald Fleming and Bernard Bailyn, *The Intellectual Migration: Europe and America, 1930–1960* (Cambridge, Ma.: Harvard University Press, 1969).
12. Gustave Von Grunebaum had many articles and books on Islamic cities and civilization, the most important being "The Structure of the Muslim Town," in *Islam: Essays in the Nature and Growth of a Cultural Tradition* (London: Routledge

and Kegan Paul, 1955).

13. Gustave Von Grunebaum, *op. cit.*, 1955, pp. 145—147.

14. *Ibid.*, p. 145.

15. *Ibid.*, p. 147 and 154.

16. Edward Said, *op. cit.*, p. 296.

17. Xavier De Planhol, *World of Islam* (Ithaca: Cornell University Press, 1959), p. 23.

18. R. Jairazbhoy, *Art and Cities of Islam* (New York: Asia Publishing House, 1965), pp. 59—60.

19. *Ibid.*, pp. 57—66.

20. Ahmed Monier has many articles in Arabic on the subject. This book, *Cities of Islam* (Beirut: B.A.U. Press, 1971), published in English, provides a summary of much of his work.

21. Adel Ismail, *Origin, Ideology and Physical Pattern of Arab Urbanization* (Karsruhe: University Dissertations, 1969); also abstracted in an article with the same title in *Ekistics*, 195 (Feb. 1972), pp. 113—123.

22. Albert Hourani and S. M. Stern, eds., *The Islamic City* (Oxford: Bruno Cassirer, 1970).

23. Albert Hourani, "The Islamic City in Light of Recent Research," in Albert Hourani and S. M. Stern, eds., *op. cit.*, pp. 9—24.

24. Nader Ardlan and Laila Bakhtiar, *The Sense of Unity* (Chicago: University of Chicago Press, 1973).

25. Heinz Gaube, *Iranian Cities* (New York: New York University Press, 1979).

26. *Ibid.*, pp. 18.

27. *Ibid.*, pp. 19—20.

28. Samuel Noe, "In Search of 'The' Traditional Islamic City: An Analytical Proposal with Lahore as a Case Example," in *Ekistics*, 280 (Jan.–Feb. 1980) pp. 69—75.

29. The main difference between Lahore and the typical Muslim city is the lack of the strict physical separation of the residential quarters in the former, a quality often present in the latter.

30. J. M. Wagstaff, "The Origin and Evolution of Towns," in G. H. Blake and R. J. Lawless, eds., *The Changing Middle Eastern City* (London: Crown Helm, 1903), pp. 11—33.

31. Besim Hakim, *Arabic-Islamic Cities* (London: KPI, 1986).

32. Max Weber, *The City*, D. Martindale and G. Newirth, trans. (Glenco, 1958).

33. Robert Brunschvig, "Urbanisme Medieval et Droit Musulmane," *Revue des Etudes Islamiques 15* (1947), pp. 127—155.

34. Louis Massignon, "Sinf," in *Encyclopedia of Islam* (London: 1956), 4, pp. 436—437.

35. Abdullah Laroui, "Pour une methodologie des etudes islamiques: L'Islam au miroir de Gustave Von Grunebaum," in *Diogene 38* (July–September, 1973); also published in Laroui's *The Crisis of the Arab Intellectual: Traditionalism or Historicism*, D. Cammell, trans. (Berkeley: University of California Press, 1976).

36. Edward Said, *op. cit.*, p. 298.

37. *Ibid.*, p. 299.

38. Gustave Von Grunebaum, 1955, *op. cit.*, p. 154.

39. Marshall Hodgson, *The Venture of Islam* (Chicago: University of Chicago Press, 1974), vol. 2, pp. 23—106.

40. Kenneth Brown, "The Uses of a Concept: The 'Muslim City'," in K. Brown, M. Jole, P. Sluglett, and S. Zubaida, eds., *Middle Eastern Cities in a Comparative Perspective* (London: Ithaca Press, 1986).

41. Claude Cahen, "Y a-t-il eu des corporations professionnellis dans le monde musulman classique," in A. Hourani and S. Stern, eds., *op. cit.*, pp. 51—63.

42. S. Goitein, *Studies in Islamic History and Institutions* (Leiden: 1966), p. 267.

43. S. M. Stern, "The Constitution of the Islamic City," in A. Hourani and S. Stern, eds., *op. cit.*, pp. 25—50.

44. Mahmoud Abdel-Rahim, "Legal Institutions," in R. B. Serjeant, ed., *The Islamic City* (Paris: UNESCO, 1980), p. 42.

45. Dale Eickelman, *The Middle East: An Anthropological Approach* (Englewood Cliffs, N.J.: Prentice-Hall, 1981).

46. Claude Cahen, *op. cit.*, pp. 51—63.

47. Jean Aubin, "Elements pour L'etude des agglomerations urbaines dans L'Iran medievel," in A. Hourani and S. Stern, eds., *op. cit.*, pp. 65—75.

48. Ira Lapidus, *Muslim Cities in the Later Middle Ages* (Cambridge, Ma.: Harvard University Press, 1967).

49. Albert Hourani, "The Islamic City in Light of Recent Research," in A. Hourani and S. Stern, eds., *op. cit.*, pp. 9—24.

50. Edward Said, *op. cit.*

51. Nader Ardlan, *op. cit.*

52. Other scholars of this group also include: Othman Llewellyn, "Shariah Values Pertaining to Landscape Planning and Design," in A. Germen, ed., *Islamic Architecture and Urbanism* (Dammam: King Faisal University Press, 1983); and Youssef Belkacem, "Bioclimatic Patterns and Human Aspects of Urban Form in the Islamic City," and Stefano Bianco, "Traditional Muslim City in Western Planning Ideologies," in I. Serageldin and S. El-Sadek, eds., *The Arab City* (Riyadh: Arab Urban Development Institute, 1982).

53. Besim Hakim, *Ibid.*; Saleh al-Hathloul, *Tradition, Continuity and Change in the Physical Environment: The Arab Muslim City* (Ann Arbor: UMI, 1981); and Jamel Akbar, *Crisis in the Built Environment: The Case of the Muslim City* (Singapore: Concept Media, 1988).

54. The proceedings of these conferences were all published in book form: R. B. Serjeant, ed., *The Islamic City* (London: UNESCO, 1980); I. Serageldin and S. El-Sadek, eds., *The Arab City* (Riyadh: Arab Urban Development Institute, 1982); A. Germen, ed., *Islamic Architecture and Urbanism* (Damman: King Faisal University, 1983); K. Brown,

M. Jole, P. Sluglett, and S. Zubaida, eds., *Middle Eastern Cities in a Comparative Perspective* (London: Ithaca Press, 1986); A. Saggaf, ed., *The Middle East City* (New York: Paragon House, 1987).

55.   Ira Lapidus, "Muslim Cities and Islamic Societies," in Ira Lapidus, ed., *Middle Eastern Cities* (Berkeley: University of California Press, 1969), p. 73.

56.   Abdul Aziz Saggaf, ed., *The Middle East City* (New York: Paragon House, 1987), p. 3.

57.   Besim Hakim, *op. cit.*, pp. 137—139.

58.   Edward Said, *op. cit.*, p. 263.

59.   *Ibid.*, p. 60.

CHAPTER III

1.   K. A. C. Creswell, *A Short Account of Early Muslim Architecture* (Beirut: Librairie du Liban, 1958).

2.   Oleg Grabar, *The Formation of Islamic Art* (New Haven: Yale University Press, 1973).

3.   Fred Donner, *The Early Islamic Conquests* (Princeton: Princeton University Press, 1981), pp. 269—271.

4.   E. A. Belyaev, *Arabs, Islam and the Arab Caliphate*, translated from Russian by A. Gourevitch (New York: Praeger, 1969); and Gustave Von Grunebaum, *Islam: Essays in the Nature of a Cultural Tradition* (London: Routledge and Kegan Paul, 1955).

5.   A. A. Duri, *Al-Takuin al Tarikh L-Lumah al-'Arabiyah* (Beirut: Markaz Derastut al-Wehdah al-Arabiyah, 1984); and M. A. Sha'aban, *Sadr al-Islam wa al-Daweah al-Amawiyah* (Beirut: Al-'Ahliyah L-Lmashr, 1983).

6.   Fred Donner, 1981, *op. cit.*, p. 270.

7.   *Ibid.*, p. 269.

8.   *Ibid.*, p. 266.

9.   Saleh al-Hathloul, *Tradition, Continuity and Change in the Physical Environment: The Arab Muslim City* (Ann Arbor: UMI, 1981), p. 21.

10.   The word *misr* means "borders" in many Semitic languages. In Arabic, the term means "urban area" and is probably pre-Islamic in origin since one can find several uses of it in the classical Arabic poetry of the Jahiliah period as a term describing the laws of the surrounding empires. I have not been able to identify the first post-Islamic instance in which the term was used. Most early historians like Yaqut, Baladhri, and Tabari use the term to mean the administrative and political role of a designated city. For more information on this subject, refer to Saleh al-Ali, *Al-Tanzimat al-Ijtema'ia wa al-Iqtesadiyah Fi al-Basrah* (Beirut: Dar al-Talia`a, 1953).

11. *Ibid.*, p. 17.
12. *Ibid.*, p. 14.
13. Ahmad Shalabi, *Musu'at al-Tarikh wa al-Hadarah al-Islamiyah* (Cairo: Maktabat al-Anglo al-Misriyah, 1974), vol. I, p. 133.
14. Mustafa al-Musawi, *Al-'Auamel al-Tarikhiyah L-nash'at wa Tatur al-Mudun al-Arabiyah al-Islamiyah* (Baghdad: Ministry of Culture, 1982), p. 67.
15. Saleh al-Ali, 1953, *op. cit.*, p. 34.
16. Ahmad al-Baladhri (279/892), *Futuh al-Buldan* (Cairo: Al-Matba'ah al-Mesriyah, 1957), p. 476.
17. Saleh al-Ali, *op. cit.*, p. 34.
18. Mustafa al-Musawi, *op. cit.*, p. 71.
19. Ahmad al-Baladhri, *op. cit.*, p. 388.
20. *Ibid.*, p. 482.
21. Abu-'Uthman al-Jahez (255/849), *Al-Baiyan wa al-Tabiyen* (Cairo: Al-Matba'ah Al-Amiyriyah, 1948), vol. 2, p. 225.
22. *Ibid.*, p. 226.
23. Mustafa al-Musawi, *op. cit.*, p. 73.
24. Abu Ja'afar al-Tabari (224/818), *Tarikh al-Rusul Wa al-Muluk* (Cairo: Dar Al-Ma'aref, 1963), vol. 4, p. 70.
25. Jamel Akbar, "Responsibility and the Traditional Muslim-Built Environment," Ph.D. dissertation (Cambridge, Ma.: MIT, 1984); later published as *Crisis in the Built Environment: The Case of the Muslim City* (Singapore: Concept Media, 1988).
26. Ahmad al-Baladhri, *op. cit.*, p. 347.
27. Ira Lapidus, "Arab Settlement and Economic Development of Iraq and Iran in the Age of the Ummayyad and Early Abbasid Caliphs," in A. L. Udovitch, ed., *The Islamic Middle East, 700–1900* (Princeton: Darwin Press, 1981) p. 182.
28. Abu-'Uthman al-Jahez, *op. cit.*, p. 262.
29. Ahmad al-Baladhri, *op. cit.*, p. 347.
30. Saleh al-Ali, *op. cit.*, pp. 266—267.
31. Saleh Lami Mustafa, *Al-Madinah al-Munawarah* (Beirut: Dar al-Nahdah al-Arabiyah, 1981).
32. 'Ali al-Mawardi (450/1039), *Al-Ahkam al-Sultaniyah* (Cairo: Dar al-Ma'aref, 1960), p. 96.
33. Ahmad al-Baladhri, *op. cit.*, p. 347.
34. Jamel Akbar, *op. cit.*, p. 164.
35. 'Ali al-Mawardi, *op. cit.*, p. 34.
36. Mustafa al-Musawi, *op. cit.*, p. 82.
37. Ahmad al-Baladhri, *op. cit.*, p. 274.
38. Khalifah ibn Khayat (340/861), *Tarikh ibn Khaiyat* (Najaf: Najaf Press, 1967), vol. I, p. 109.

39. Ahmad al-Baladhri, *op. cit.*, p. 276.
40. This is my translation of what is related by al-Baladhri (*op. cit.*, p. 276) regarding this issue. A similar quote may also be found in al-Tabari and ibn al-Athiyr, but should translate "the land that is not good for camels is not good for Arabs too."
41. Mustafa al-Musawi, *op. cit.*, p. 87.
42. *Ibid.*, p. 85.
43. Abdul-Rahman ibn Khaldun (808/1406), *Tarikh al-'Ibar* (Beirut: Dar al-Nahdah, 1959), vol. 2, p. 342.
44. Abu Ja'afar al-Tabari, *op. cit.*, vol. 4, p. 44.
45. 'Ali ibn al-'Athiyr (630/1223), *Al-Kamel Fi al-Tarikh* (Cairo: Dar al-Ketab, 1960), vol. 2, p. 411—412.
46. Abu Ja'afar al-Tabari, *op. cit.*, vol. 4, p. 45.
47. *Ibid.*
48. Saleh al-Hathloul, *op. cit.*, p. 36.
49. Abu Ja'afar al-Tabari, *op. cit.*, vol. 4, p. 46.
50. Ahmad al-Baladhri, *op. cit.*, p. 275.
51. Abu Ja'afar al-Tabari, *op. cit.*, vol. 4, p. 46.
52. *Ibid.*
53. *Ibid.*
54. K. A. C. Creswell, *op. cit.*, p. 9.
55. For more illustrations on this and others, refer to Helen and Richard Leacroft, *The Buildings of Early Islam* (Reading, Pa.: Addison Wesley, 1979), p. 3.
56. Abu Ja'afar al-Tabari, *op. cit.*, p. 47.
57. Ahmad al-Ya'aqubi (284/897), *Ketab al-Buldan* (Leiden: E. J. Brill, 1860), p. 95.
58. Abu Ja'afar al-Tabari, *op. cit.*, p. 45.
59. *Ibid.*
60. Louis Massignon, "Explication du plan de Kufa," in *Melange Maspero* (Paris: 1937), pp. 336—360.
61. Kazem al-Janabi, *Takhtit Madinat al-Kufah* (Baghdad: Ministry of Culture, 1967).
62. Jamel Akbar, *op. cit.*, p. 163.
63. Abu Ja'afar al-Tabari, *op. cit.*, p. 45.
64. Jamel Akbar, *op. cit.*, p. 60.
65. Ahmad al-Baladhri, *op. cit.*, p. 275.
66. Jamel Akbar, *op. cit.*, p. 60.
67. Abu Ja'afar al-Tabari, *op. cit.*, p. 47.
68. Ahmad al-Ya'aqubi, *op. cit.*, p. 45.
69. Abu Ja'afar al-Tabari, *op. cit.*, p. 45.
70. For more information on this process, refer to the work of John Turner and Horacio Caminos.
71. Jurji Zaydan, *Tarikh al-Tamadun al-Islami* (Cairo: Al-Helal Press, 1904), vol. 3, p. 107.
72. This could be observed in most of the chronicles including al-Baladhri, *op. cit.*;

al-Tabari, *op. cit.*; and al-Ya'aqubi, *op. cit.*

73.   Mustafa al-Musawi, *op. cit.*

74.   Michael Morony, *Iraq After the Muslim Conquest* (Princeton: Princeton University Press, 1984), p. 32.

75.   El-Sayed A. Salem, *Tarikh al-Dawlah al-Arabiyah* (Beirut: Dar al-Nahdah, 1986).

76.   E. A. Belayaev, *op. cit.*, p. 130.

77.   El-Sayed A. Salem, *op. cit.*, p. 275.

78.   E. A. Belayaev, *op. cit.*, pp. 130—149; and Ira Lapidus, "The Evolution of Early Muslim Urban Society," in *Comparative Studies in Society and History* 15, no. 1 (January 1973), pp. 21—50.

79.   Al-Sayed Salem, *op. cit.*; and R. B. Serjeant, *The Islamic City* (Paris: UNESCO, 1980).

80.   Philip Hitti, *Capital Cities of Arab Islam* (Minneapolis: University of Minnesota Press, 1973), p. 46.

81.   This story is reported in three slightly varying forms by al-Mas'udi, *Muruj Al-Dhahab* (Cairo: 1942), vol. 2, p. 332; Ibn Khaldun, *Al-Muqaddemah* (Cairo: 1938); and Ibn Qutaiybah, *Al-Imamah Wa al-Siasah* (Cairo: 1945), p. 33.

82.   Abu Ja'afar al-Tabari, *op. cit.*, vol. 5, p. 134.

83.   El-Sayed A. Salem, *op. cit.*, p. 293.

84.   Martin Hinds, "Kufan Political Alignments and Their Background in the Mid 7th Century," in *International Journal of Middle Eastern Studies,* vol. 2, no. 1 (1971), pp. 346—367.

85.   For more details on this issue refer to al-Baladhri, *op. cit.*, and al-Tabari, *op. cit.*

86.   Reported by Abu-Ja'afar al-Tabari, *op. cit.*, vol. 4, p. 193; and al-Mas'udi, *op. cit.*, vol. 2, p. 334.

87.   Abu Ja'afar al-Tabari, *op. cit.*, vol. 5, p. 134.

88.   Philip Hitti, *op. cit.*, p. 48.

89.   Martin Hinds, *op. cit.*, p. 351.

90.   Oleg Grabar, *op. cit.*, p. 30.

91.   The chronicles indicate that different cities had different names for the same type of space. *Sahn, Sahah,* and *Rahbah* were the common names designating the central square of a garrison town.

92.   Saleh al-Hathloul, *op. cit.*, p. 41.

93.   Jurji Zaydan, *op. cit.*, p. 69.

94.   Michael Morony, *op. cit.*, p. 73.

95.   El-Sayed A. Salem, *op. cit.*, p. 314.

CHAPTER IV

1.   Philip Hitti, *Capital Cities of Arab Islam* (Minneapolis: University of Minnesota Press, 1973), p. 142.

2. Oleg Grabar, *The Formation of Islamic Art* (New Haven: Yale University Press, 1973), p. 85.

3. Kamal Salibi, *Syria Under Islam* (New York: Caravan Books, 1977), p. 26.

4. I chose to highlight the story of Damascus instead of any other Syrian town because Damascus was a seat of government. Jerusalem, which is well documented, would have provided a slightly different picture of Arab building activity but it remains a relatively unique city more reflective of architectural than of urban efforts. For more details on the conquest of Damascus, refer to the work of Donner and Wellhausen.

5. Ahmad al-Baladhri (279/892), *Futuh al-Buldan* (Cairo: Al-Matba'ah al-Mesriyah, 1957), p. 129.

6. Abu Ja'afar al-Tabari (224/818), *Tarikh al-Rusul Wa al-Muluk* (Cairo: Dar Al-Ma'aref, 1963), vol. 3, p. 440.

7. Nikita Elisseeff, "Dimashk," in *Encyclopedia of Islam* (Leiden: E. J. Brill, 1965), vol. 2, p. 280.

8. *Ibid.*

9. *Ibid.*

10. *Ibid.*

11. Ahmad Sabanum, *Demashq Fi Dawa'er al-Ma'aref* (Damascus: Dar al-Ketab al-Arabi, 1986), pp. 45—48.

12. The antagonism between Caliph 'Umar and Commander Khaled has been the subject of extensive writings. 'Abas al-'Aqad's classic Arabic books *The Genius of Umar, The Genius of Khaled,* and *Umar and Khaled* are good accounts of this subject.

13. Nikita Elisseeff, "Demashk," in *op. cit.*, p. 280.

14. Fred Donner, *The Early Islamic Conquests* (Princeton: Princeton University Press, 1981), p. 246.

15. *Ibid.*

16. *Ibid.*, p. 245.

17. *Ibid.*, p. 249.

18. Jurji Zaydan, *Tarikh al-Tamadun al-Islami* (Cairo: Al-Helal Press, 1904), vol. 3, p. 54.

19. Nikita Elisseeff, "Demansk," in *op. cit.*, p. 280.

20. *Ibid.*

21. Jean Sauvaget, "Le Plan Antique de Damas," in *Syria* 26 (1949), pp. 314—358.

22. *Ibid.*

23. Abdul Kader al-Rihawi, *Madinat Demashq* (Damascus: Al-Majaz, 1969), pp. 47—53; and Adel Ismail, *Origin, Ideology and Physical Pattern of Arab Urbanization* (Karsruhe: University Dissertations, 1969), p. 70.

24. Jean Sauvaget, *op. cit.*, 1949, pp. 314—358; and Adel Ismail, 1969, *op. cit.*, p. 70.

25. Fred Donner, *op. cit.*, p. 246.

26. Abu Ja'afar al-Tabari, *op. cit.*, vol. 1, p. 2159; Yaqut al-Hamawi, *Mujama'a Al-*

Buldan (Beirut: Dar al-Nahdah, 1956), p. 147; and Khalifa ibn Khayat, *Tarikh ibn Khayat* (Baghdad: 1951), vol. 1, p. 94.

27. Fred Donner, *op. cit.*, p. 247, based on a comparative examination of the texts of al-Tabari, al-Baladhri, and Khalifa.
28. *Ibid.*, p. 245.
29. Nikita Elisseeff, *op. cit.*, 281, based on ibn Jubair.
30. *Ibid.*, based on P. Gayer, *Itinera Hierosolymitana* Saeculi iv-viii, pp. 4—8.
31. De Geoje and Von Kremer were both cited in K. A. C. Creswell, *A Short Account of Early Muslim Architecture* (Beirut: Librairie du Liban, 1958), p. 65.
32. *Ibid*, p. 72.
33. Nikita Elisseeff, *op. cit.*, p. 277.
34. Saleh L. Mustafa, *Al-Madinah al-Munawarah* (Beirut: Dar al-Nahdah al-Arabiyah, 1981), pp. 11—15.
35. Philip Hitti, *op. cit.*, p. 65.
36. *Ibid.*, p. 66.
37. *Ibid.*, p. 66.
38. Muhamad ibn Manzur (711/1310), *Mukhtasar Tarikh Demashq L-ibn 'Asaker* (Damascus: Dar al-Fekr, 1984), pp. 292—293.
39. Saleh L. Mustafa, *op. cit.*, p. 11—15.
40. 'Ali ibn 'Asaker (571/1175), *Tarikh Demashq* (Damascus: Al-Majma'a al-'Ilmi, 1952), vol. 1, p. 134.
41. *Ibid.*
42. Nikita Elisseeff, *op. cit.*, p. 280.
43. Philip Hitti, *op. cit.*, p. 280.
44. Salah al-Munjid, *Tarikh Madinat Demashq* (Damascus: Dar al-Ketab, 1961).
45. Jean Sauvaget, "Esquisse d'une histoire de la ville de Damas," in *Revue Etudes Islamiques*, vol. 3, 1934, pp. 441—452.
46. Xavier De Planhol, *World of Islam* (Ithaca: Cornell University Press, 1959), p. 15.
47. Gustave Von Grunebaum, *Islam: Essays in the Nature and Growth of a Cultural Tradition* (London: Routledge and Kegan Paul, 1955), p. 149.
48. K. A. C. Creswell, *op. cit.*, concludes that the Maqsura must have been introduced during Muawiyah's reign in spite of Lammen's refutations.
49. Philip Hitti, *op. cit.*, p. 76.
50. Nikita Elisseeff, *op. cit.*, p. 280.
51. Muhammad Ibn Manzur, *op. cit.*, p. 261.
52. *Ibid.*, p. 262.
53. K. A. C. Creswell, *op. cit.*, pp. 60—62.
54. *Ibid.*, p. 68.
55. Muhamad Ibn Manzur, *op. cit.*, p. 264.
56. *Ibid.*
57. *Ibid.*, p. 265.

58. *Ibid.*, p. 267.
59. *Ibid.*, p. 268.
60. *Ibid.*
61. *Ibid.*
62. *Ibid.*, p. 269.
63. Ali ibn 'Asaker, *op. cit.*, vol. 2, p. 33.
64. *Ibid.*
65. *Ibid.*
66. K. A. C. Creswell, *op. cit.*, p. 94.
67. The theory about the reluctant conversion of the early Arabs from nomadic to sedentary urban life has been challenged by many scholars; as far as the chronicled evidence is concerned, it can not be substantiated. For a more detailed discussion of the idea of desert palaces as self-sufficient communities, refer to Oleg Grabar in several articles and books, most notably: "Three Seasons of Excavations at Qasr Al-Hayr Al-Sharqi," *Ars Orientalis*, 8 (1970), pp. 65—85; and then later in his "The Formation of Islamic Art," *op. cit.*, pp. 132—177. Grabar's views on the subject may also be found in *City in the Desert*, with Renata Holod, Jane Knustad, and William Trousdale (Cambridge, Ma.: Harvard Middle East Monographs, 1978); and more recently in *The Art and Architecture of Islam*, with Richard Ettinghausen (New York: Pelican History of Art — Pelican Books, 1987), pp. 45—67.
68. Muhamad 'Azimi, *Tarikh Halab* (Damascus, 1984).
69. Jean Sauvaget, 1939, *op. cit.*
70. Saleh L. Mustafa, *op. cit.*
71. Jean Sauvaget, *Alep* (Paris: Librairie Orientaliste, 1941), p. 74.
72. Adel Ismail, *Origin, Ideology and Physical Pattern of Arab Urbanization* (Karsruhe: University Dissertations, 1969), p. 70.
73. Jean Sauvaget, 1941, *op. cit.*, p. 79.
74. Adel Ismail, *op. cit.*, p. 70.
75. *Ibid.* Based on Sauvaget, 1941.
76. *Ibid.*
77. *Ibid.*
78. El Sayed A. Salem, *Tarikh al-Maghreb al-Kabir* (Beirut: Dar al-Nahdah al-Arabiyah, 1981), p. 273.
79. *Ibid.*
80. Kamal Salibi, *op. cit.*, p. 33.
81. *Ibid.*
82. Philip Hitti, *op. cit.*, p. 138.
83. *Ibid.*
84. *Ibid.*, p. 141.
85. *Ibid.*, p. 144.
86. Ahmad ibn Udhri (700/1300), *Al-Baiyan fi Akhbar al-Maghreb* (Beirut: Dar Sader,

1950), vol. 2, p. 378; Ahmad al-Maqqri, *Nahi al-Tayb* (Cairo, 1949), vol. 1, pp. 217—218.

87. *Ibid.*
88. El-Sayed A. Salem, *op. cit.*
89. Philip Hitti, *op. cit.*, p. 130.
90. Oleg Grabar, "The Architecture of the Middle Eastern City," in Ira Lapidus, ed., *Middle Eastern Cities* (Berkeley: University of California Press, 1969), p. 73.
91. Oleg Grabar, *op. cit.*, 1973, pp. 119—120.
92. Fred Donner, *op. cit.*

CHAPTER V

1. Ira Lapidus, "Traditional Muslim Cities: Structure and Change," in L. Carl Brown, ed., *From Madina to Metropolis* (Princeton: Darwin Press, 1973), p. 52.
2. Jacob Lassner, "The Caliph's Personal Domain," in A. Hourani and S. M. Stern, eds., *The Islamic City* (Oxford: Bruno Cassirer, 1970), p. 103.
3. John Glubb, *A Short History of the Arab Peoples* (New York: Stein and Day, 1969), p. 9.
4. El Sayed A. Salem, *Al-Tarikh al-Siyasi wa al-Hadari Ll-Dawlah al-Arabiyah* (Beirut: Dar al-Nahdah, 1987), pp. 351—356.
5. John Grubb, *op. cit.*, p. 91.
6. *Ibid.*, p. 93.
7. Kamal Salibi, *Syria Under Islam* (New York: Caravan Books, 1977), p. 33.
8. Philip Hitti, *Capital Cities of Arab Islam* (Minneapolis: University of Minnesota Press, 1973), p. 86.
9. El-Sayed A. Salem, *op. cit.*, 1987, p. 581.
10. Reuben Levy, *A Baghdad Chronicle* (Cambridge: Cambridge University Press, 1929), p. 14.
11. Jacob Lassner, *The Shaping of Abbasid Rule* (Princeton: Princeton University Press, 1980), p. 159.
12. *Ibid.*, p. 160.
13. Reuben Levy, *op. cit.*, p. 15.
14. Abu Ja'afar al-Tabari (d. 224/818), *Tarikh al-Rusul Wa al-Muluk* (Cairo: Dar al-Ma'aref, 1963), vol. 3, p. 274.
15. Abu Ja'afar al-Tabari, *op. cit.*, vol. 1, pp. 271—275; Ahmad al-Ya'aqubi (284/897), *Ketab al-Buldan* (Leiden, 1892) pp. 8—23; and Yaqut al-Hamawi, *Mujma'a al-Buldan* (Leipzig, 1866), vol. 1, pp. 674—680.
16. Al-Khatib al-Baghdadi (463/1071), *Tarikh Baghdad* (Cairo: al-Matba'ah al-Mesriyah, 1931), vol. 1, p. 66; Yaqut al-Hamawi, *op. cit.*, vol. 1, p. 680; and Abu Ja'afar al-Tabari, *op. cit.*, p. 165.

17. Jacob Lassner, 1980, *op. cit.*, p. 165.
18. *Ibid.*, p. 168.
19. Al-Khatib al-Baghdadi, *op. cit.*, vol. 1, pp. 66—67.
20. Jacob Lassner, 1970, in A. Hourani and S. M. Stern, ed., *op. cit.*, p. 68.
21. Ahmad al-Ya'aqubi, *op. cit.*, vol. 2, p. 430.
22. Abu Ja'afar al-Tabari, *op. cit.*, vol. 7, p. 618.
23. *Ibid.*
24. Ahmad al-Ya'aqubi, *op. cit.*, vol. 2, p. 238.
25. Abu Ja'afar al-Tabari, *op. cit.*, vol. 2, p. 238.
26. *Ibid*, vol. 3, p. 320.
27. *Ibid.*
28. Saleh El-Ali, "The Foundation of Baghdad," in A. Hourani and S. M. Stern, *op. cit.*, pp. 88—89.
29. Jacob Lassner, 1980, *op. cit.*, pp. 194—196.
30. K. A. C. Creswell, *A Short Account of Early Muslim Architecture* (Beirut: Librairie du Liban, 1958), p. 174.
31. For a detailed discussion on the naming of Baghdad, refer to Mustafa al-Musawi, *Al-'Awamel al-Tarikhiyah L-nasha'at wa Tatur al-Mudun al-Arabiyah al-Islamiyah* (Baghdad: Ministry of Culture, 1982) p. 137.
32. J. M. Rogers, "Samarra," in A. Hourani and S. M. Stern, *op. cit.*, p. 128.
33. Saleh El-Ali, *op. cit.*, p. 93.
34. Jacob Lassner, *The Topography of Baghdad in the Early Middle Ages* (Detroit: Wayne State University Press, 1970), p. 52.
35. *Ibid.*
36. For a detailed discussion about the cosmological argument and its effect on Islamic architectural form, refer to Nader Ardlan and Lale Bakhtiar, *The Sense of Unity* (Chicago: University of Chicago Press, 1973).
37. K. A. C. Creswell, *op. cit.*, p. 179.
38. Guy LeStrange, *Baghdad During the Abbasid Caliphate* (Oxford: Clarendon Press, 1900), p. 34, plus accompanying maps.
39. Jacob Lassner, 1980, *op. cit.*, pp. 194—196.
40. Ahmad al-Ya'aqubi, *op. cit.*, vol. 2, p. 238.
41. Al-Khatib al-Baghdadi, *op. cit.*, vol. 1, pp. 71—73.
42. Oleg Grabar, *The Formation of Islamic Art* (New Haven: Yale University Press, 1973), p. 66.
43. Guy LeStrange, *op. cit.*, p. 15.
44. E. Herzfeld, *Archaologische Reise im Euphrat und Tigris Gebiet* (Berlin, 1921), vol. 2, p. 137.
45. Philip Hitti, *op. cit.*, p. 87.
46. Jacob Lassner, 1980, *op. cit.*, p. 190.
47. Saleh al-Hathloul, *Tradition, Continuity and Change in the Physical Environment:*

The Arab Muslim City (Ann Arbor: UMI, 1981), p. 46. This does not necessarily contradict O. Grabar's view in *op. cit.*, that the round form started to merge with the rest of the city even during al-Mansur's reign.

48. Ahmad al-Ya'aqubi, *op. cit.*, pp. 14—23.
49. Jacob Lassner, 1980, *op. cit.*, pp. 184—197.
50. Saleh El-Ali, *op. cit.*, p. 151; and Jacob Lassner, 1980, *op. cit.*, pp. 194—196.
52. Saleh El-Ali, *op. cit.*, p. 101.
53. Al-Kahtib al-Baghdadi, *op. cit.*, vol. 1, pp. 79—80.
54. *Ibid.*, vol. 1, p. 78; Abu Ja'afar al-Tabari, *op. cit.*, vol. 3, p. 323; and Yaqut al-Hamawi, *op. cit.*, vol. 4, p. 254.
55. Jacob Lassner, 1980, *op. cit.*, p. 195.
56. *Ibid.*
57. Reuben Levy, *op. cit.*, p. 30.
58. Al-Kahtib al-Baghdadi, *op. cit.*, vol. 1, pp. 75—80; and Ahmad al-Ya'aqubi, *op. cit.*, p. 245.
59. Jacob Lassner, 1980, *op. cit.*, p. 80.
60. Abdel Aziz Duri,"Government Institutions," in R. B. Serjeant, ed., *The Islamic City* (Paris: UNESCO, 1980), p. 57.
61. Mustafa al-Musawi, *op. cit.*, p. 138.
62. Abdel Aziz Duri, *op. cit.*, p. 57.
63. Janet Abu-Lughod, *Cairo: 1001 Years of the City Victorious* (Princeton: Princeton University Press, 1971), p. 16.
64. Philip Hitti, *op. cit.*, p. 110.
65. Janet Abu-Lughod, *op. cit.*, p. 18.
66. Marcel Clerget, *Le Caire* (Cairo: Imprimerie E & R Schindler, 1934), vol. 1, p. 128.
67. Janet Abu-Lughod, *op. cit.*, p. 18.
68. Philip Hitti, *op. cit.*, p. 18.
69. Abdul Rahman Zaki, *Al-Qahirah 969—1825* (Cairo: Al-Dar al-Mesriyah L-Lta'lif wa al-Targamah, 1966), p. 10.
70. Ahmad al-Maqrizi (846/1442), *Al-Mawa'aez wa al'I'tibar Fi Zikr al-Khutat wa al-Athar* (Cairo: Bulaq Press, 1855), vol. 2, p. 179.
71. Abdul Rahman Zaki, *op. cit.*, p. 10.
72. *Ibid.*
73. Marcel Clerget, *op. cit.*, vol. 7, p. 123.
74. C. J. Haswell, "Cairo: Origin and Development," in *Bulletin de la Societe Royal de Geographie d'Egypte*, vols. 3 and 4, 1933, p. 176.
75. Roger LeTourneau in an interview with Janet Abu-Lughod, published as footnote in *op. cit.*, p. 18.
76. R. Reitemeyer, *Beschreibung Agyptens* (Leipzig, 1903), p. 261.
77. Ahmad al-Maqrizi, *op. cit.*, vol. 2, p. 273.
78. Nezar AlSayyad, *Streets of Islamic Cairo* (Cambridge, Ma.: Aga Khan Program

for Islamic Architecture, 1981), p. 16.

79. Ahmad al-Maqrizi, *op. cit.*, vol. 2, p. 275.

80. Philip Hitti, *op. cit.*, p. 114.

81. Ahmad al-Maqrizi, *op. cit.*, vol. 1, p. 377.

82. Ali Mubarak, *Al-Khutat al-Tawfiqiyah al-Jadidah* (Cairo: Dar al-Kutub, 1969), vol. 1, p. 42.

83. *Ibid.*, vol. 1, p. 36.

84. Ahmad Al-Maqrizi, *op. cit.*, vol. 2, p. 273.

85. Abdul Rahman Zaki rightfully downplays the importance of the mosques of Amr and Ibn Touloun that continued to accommodate Friday congregations on the basis that they were located at a considerable walking distance from Al-Qahirah and because they continued the Sunni Khutbah instead of the official shi'it one sanctioned by the Fatimid caliphs.

86. Yaacov Lev, "Army, Regime and Society in Fatimid Egypt, 968–1094," in *International Journal of Middle Eastern Studies*, vol. 19, no. 3 (August, 1987), pp. 337–366.

87. Ali-Mubarak, *op. cit.*, vol. 1, p. 44.

88. Ahmad al-Maqrizi, *op. cit.*, vol. 2, p. 245.

89. *Ibid.*

90. Abdul Rahman Zaki, *op. cit.*, p. 20.

91. *Ibid.*, p. 25.

92. Ali Mubarak, *op. cit.*, vol. 1, p. 46.

93. Nasiri Khusraw, *Safar Nameh*, translated from Persian to Arabic by Y. al-Chashab (Cairo: Lagnat al-Ta'alif wa Nashr, 1945), p. 48.

94. For a more detailed discussion on the disintegration of the regular Fatimid plan close to the end of their rule, refer to Nezar AlSayyad, "Space in an Islamic City," in *Journal of Architectural and Planning Research* (Chicago: Locke Science Publishing Co., 1987), vol. 4, no. 2, pp. 108–119; and Nezar AlSayyad, *op. cit.*, 1981.

APPENDIX A:
TRANSLITERATION AND DATES

SYSTEM OF TRANSLITERATION

The system of transliteration used in this book is a modified version of the Encyclopedia of Islam system. English quotations borrowed from other texts were left they way the appeared in their original texts. Common words found in English dictionaries and proper names of contemporary cities, scholars, or subjects were also revised according to the conventions of the related countries or disciplines; all other names follow the system mentioned below. The *al* in frequently used proper names will appear only in the first occurrence.

١	ب	ت	ث	ج	ح	خ	د	ذ	ر	ز	س	ش
A	B	T	Th	J	h	kh	D	DH	R	Z	S	Sh
a	b	t	th	j	H	Kh	d	dh	r	z	s	Sh

ص	ض	ط	ظ	ع	غ	ف	ق	ك	ل	م	ن	ه
S	d	T	Z	'	GH	F	Q	K	L	M	N	H
S	D	t	z	'	gh	f	q	k	l	m	n	h

ة	و	و	ي	ى	ﻱ	ى	إ	ال	́	̕	̓	'
-	W	U	-	-	y	-	I	-	-	-	-	'
h	w	u	iy	i	-	a	-	al	a	u	e	'

DATES AND PERIODS

Depending on the subject matter of each individual chapter, I will switch from the Gregorian Calendar (A.D.) to the Hijri Calendar (H). In dealing with the work of contemporary scholars, Arabs or Europeans, I will use the Gregorian dates (for example, 1904 A.D.). In dealing with historical subjects, I will use the Hijri date (for example, 497 H). In particular situations, where comparisons are necessary, I will give both dates (for example, 497/1104) with the Hijri year appearing first. Because of the differences between these two calendars, (one solar and the other lunar), the spread is usually variable. According to the *New Columbia Encyclopedia*, the first Hijri year began on Friday, July 16, 622 A.D.

APPENDIX B:
GLOSSARY

Ahl:	Family
'Amel Al-Suq:	Market supervisor
Amir:	Literally, Prince, but often used to mean governor of city or region
Amsar (sing. *Misr*):	Settlements designated as administrative centers
Ansar:	Adherents and followers of the prophet
Baiyt (pl. *buyut*):	A residence
Baiyt Al-Mal:	Public treasury
Dar:	A residence or a house
Dar Al-Hikmah:	House of wisdom
Dar Al-'Ilm:	House of science
Dar Al-Imarah:	The governor's office or residence
Dar Al-Islam:	The abode of Islam; territories in which the shariah prevails
Dar Al-Khalifah:	Residence and office of the caliph
Darb (pl. *Durub*):	Lane
Figh:	Jurisprudence
Fina:	An enclosed open space or courtyard
Fustat:	Army encampment
Hadith:	Saying of the prophet
Harah:	Residential quarter
Hijrah:	The Islamic calendar marking the emigration of the prophet from Mecca to Madinah in 622 A.D.
Ibn:	Son of . . .
Ijma'a:	Consensus of opinion
Ikhlat (sing. *Khilt*):	A grouping of individuals belonging to different tribes

Juma'ah:	Friday
Khalifah:	Caliph
Khutat (sing. *Khutah*):	Plans marked out on the land; also referring to collective holdings
Kanisah:	Church
Khutbah:	The Friday sermon
Madrasah:	School
Mahal:	Residential quarter
Majles:	Court
Malek:	King
Manahej:	Road system
Manzel (pl. *Manazel*):	House or houses
Marbad:	Halting place or way station
Maiydan:	Public square or open space
Mu'alem:	Master craftsman
Muhandes:	Master builder or engineer
Muhtaseb:	Market official
Mujahedin:	Fighters for Islam
Musalah:	An open place set aside for prayer
Qadi:	judge
Qasr:	Palace
Qatai'a:	Fief, land granted by feudal tenure
Qibla:	Direction of prayer towards Mecca
Rabad:	Quarter
Rabbah:	Open space or public square surrounded by buildings
Rashedun:	Term used to designate the orthodox caliphs
Rawadef (sing. *Radeef*):	Later immigrants to a city
Rebat:	Defensive post
Sahah:	Open space or yard
Sahn:	Courtyard of house or mosque
Shari'a:	Islamic law
Sikah (pl. *Sikak*):	Side streets
Suq (pl. *Aswaq*):	Market
Tariq:	Road
Waqf:	An endowment of land or building
Waley/Wazir:	Governor
Zuqaq:	Lanes and alleys

APPENDIX C:
FIGURES AND CREDITS

All figures in this book are by the author, who acknowledges the authors and editors of several books and articles from which textual or visual material served as a basis for some of the illustrations in this book. Credit is given to those individuals or institutions as their names appear following the picture captions. Unless otherwise is indicated, North is at the top of the page on all maps and diagrams. Illustrations are only diagrams when no scale accompanies them.

BIBLIOGRAPHY

PRIMARY SOURCES

al-Baghdadi, Al-Kahtib (463/1071). *Tarikh Baghdad* (Cairo: Al-Matba'ah al-Mesriyah, 1931).

al-Baladhri, Ahmad (279/892). *Futuh al-Buldan* (Cairo: Al-Matba'ah al-Mesriyah, 1957).

al-Hamawi, Yaqut. *Mujama'a al-Buldan* (Beirut: Dar al-Nahdah, 1956).

Ibn Abdul-Hakam, A. (257/871). *Futuah Mesr* (Leiden: E. J. Brill, 1860).

Ibn al-'Athiyr, 'Ali (630/1223). *Al-Kamel Fi al-Tarikh* (Cairo: Dar al Ketab, 1960).

Ibn 'Asaker, 'Ali (571/1175). *Tarikh Demashq* (Damascus: al-Majma'a al-'Ilmi, 1952).

Ibn Khaldun, Abdul-Rahman (808/1406). Tarikh al-'Ibar (Beirut: Dar al-Nahdah, 1959).
————. *Al-Muqaddemah* (Cairo: 1938).

Ibn Khayat, Khalifah (340/861). *Tarikh Ibn Khaiyat* (Najaf: Najaf Press, 1967).

Ibn Manzur, Muhamad (711/1310). *Mukhtasar Tarikh Demashq L-Ibn 'Asaker* (Damascus: Dar al-Fekr, 1984).

Ibn Qutaiybah, A. *Al-Imamah Wa al-Siasah* (Cairo: 1945).

Ibn Udhri, Ahmad (700/1300). *Al-Baiyan fi Akhbar al-Maghreb* (Beirut: Dar Sadar, 1950).

al-Jahez, Abu-'Uthman (255/849). *Al-Baiyan wa al-Tabiyen* (Cairo: Al-Matba'ah Al-Amiriyah, 1948).

al-Maqqri, Ahmad. *Nahi al-Tayb* (Cairo, 1949).

al-Maqrizi, Ahmad (846/1442). *Al-Mawa'aez wa al-I'tibar Fi Zikr al-Khutat wa al-Athar* (Cairo: Bulaq Press, 1855).

al-Mas'udi, Ahmad. *Muruj al-Dhahab* (Cairo: 1942).

al-Mawardi, 'Ali (450/1039). *Al-Ahkam al-Sultaniyah* (Cairo: Dar al-Ma'aref, 1960).

al-Tabari, Abu Ja'afar (224/849). *Tarikh al-Rusul Wa al-Muluk* (Cairo: Dar al-Ma'aref, 1963).

al-Ya'aqubi, Ahmad (284/897). *Ketab al-Buldan* (Leiden: E. J. Brill, 1860).

Khusraw, Nasiri. *Safar Nameh*, translated from Persian to Arabic by Y. al-Chashab (Cairo: Lagnat al-Ta'lif wa Nashr, 1945).

Mubarak, Ali. *Al-Khutat al-Tawfiqiyah al-Jadidah* (Cairo: Dar al-Kutub, 1969).

SECONDARY SOURCES

Abdel-Rahim, Mahmoud, "Legal Institutions." In *The Islamic City*, R. B. Serjeant, ed. (Paris: UNESCO, 1980).

Abu-Lughod, Janet. *Cairo: 1001 Years of the City Victorious* (Princeton: Princeton University Press, 1971).

──────. "Contemporary Relevance of Islamic Urban Principles." In *Islamic Architecture and Urbanism*, A. Germen, ed. (Dammam: King Faisal University, 1983).

──────. "The Islamic City—Historic Myth, Islamic Essence and Contemporary Relevance," *International Journal of Middle East Studies 19*, no. 2, May 1987.

Adams, Robert. *Land Behind Baghdad* (Chicago: University of Chicago Press, 1965).

Akbar, Jamel. "Responsibility and the Traditional Muslim-Built Environment," Ph.D. dissertation (Cambridge, Ma.: MIT, 1984). Later published as *Crisis in the Built Environment: The Case of the Muslim City* (Singapore: Concept Media, 1988).

AlSayyad, Nezar. "Dualities in the Study of Traditional Environments." In *Dwellings, Settlements and Tradition*, Jean Paul Bourdier and Nezar AlSayyad, eds. (Lanham & London: University Press of America, 1989).

──────. "Arab Muslim Cities." *Design Book Review 14*, Spring 1988.

──────. "Urban Space in an Islamic City." In *Journal of Architectural and Planning Research 4* no. 2 (Chicago: Locke Science Publishing Co., 1987) .

──────. "Notes on the Muslim City: Physical Aspects." In *The Cost of Not Knowing: Proceedings of the 1986 EDRA Conference*, J. Wineman, R. Barnes, and C. Zimrig, eds. (Madison: Omnipress, 1986).

──────. *Streets of Islamic Cairo* (Cambridge, Ma: Aga Khan Program for Islamic Architecture, 1981).

AlSayyad, Nezar and Guita Boostani. "Mosques: The Religious Architecture of Islam." In *Encyclopedia of Architecture*, Joseph Wilkes, ed. (New York: John Wiley and Sons), vol. 8, 1989.

AlSayyad, Nezar, Kate Bristol, and S. F. Lin. "Interpreting the Form of Urban Space: Open Space and Urban Activity in a Cross-Cultural Context." In *Public Environments: Proceedings of the 1987 EDRA Conference*, Joan Harvey and Don Henning, eds. (EDRA Publications, 1987).

Ardlan, Nader and Laila Bakhtiar. *The Sense of Unity* (Chicago: University of Chicago Press, 1973).

Aubin, Jean. "Elements pour L'etude des agglomerations urbaines dans L'Iran medieval." In *The Islamic City*, A. Hourani and S. Stern, eds. (Oxford: Bruno Cassirer, 1970).

Azimi, Muhammad. *Tarikh Halab* (Damascus: Manshurat, 1984).

Belkacem, Youssef. "Bioclimatic Patterns and Human Aspects of Urban Form in the Islamic City." In *The Arab City*, I. Serageldin and S. El-Sadek, eds. (Riyadh: Arab Urban Development Institute, 1982).

Belyaev, E. A. *Arabs, Islam and the Arab Caliphate*. Translated from the Russian by A.

Gourevitch (New York: Praeger, 1969).

Benet, F. "The Ideology of Islamic Urbanization." In *Urbanization and Urbanism*, N. Anderson, ed. (London: E. J. Brill, 1964).

Berque, Jacques. "Medinas, Villesnueves et Bidonvilles." In *Les Cahiers de Tunisie*, J. Berque, ed. (Tunis, 1958).

Bianco, Stefano. "Traditional Muslim City in Western Planning Ideologies." In *The Arab City*, I. Serageldin and S. El-Sadek, eds. (Riyadh: Arab Urban Development Institute, 1982).

Brown, Kenneth. "The Uses of a Concept: the 'Muslim City'." In *Middle Eastern Cities in a Comparative Perspective*, K. Brown, M. Jole, P. Sluglett, and S. Zubaida, eds. (London: Ithaca Press, 1986).

Brown, K., M. Jole, P. Sluglett, and S. Zubaida, eds. *Middle Eastern Cities in a Comparative Perspective* (London: Ithaca Press, 1986).

Brown, L. Carl, ed. *From Madina to Metropolis* (Princeton: Darwin Press, 1973).

Brunschvig, Robert. "Urbanisme Medieval et Droit Musulmane." In *Revue des Etudes Islamiques 15* (1947).

Cahen, Claude. "Y a-t-il eu des corporations professionnellis dans le monde musulman classique." In *The Islamic City*, A. Hourani and S. Stern, eds. (Oxford: Bruno Cassirer, 1970).

Carter, Harold. *Introduction to Urban Historical Geography* (London: Edward Arnold Ltd., 1983).

Claval, Paul. "Reflections on the Cultural Geography of the European City." In *The City in Cultural Context*, J. Agnew, J. Mercer, and D. Sopher, eds. (Boston: Allen and Unwin, 1984).

Clerget, Marcel. *Le Caire* (Cairo: Imprimerie E & R Schindler, 1934).

Creswell, K. A. C. *A Short Account of Early Muslim Architecture* (Beirut: Librairie du Liban, 1958).

De Planhol, Xavier. *World of Islam* (Ithaca: Cornell University Press, 1959).

Deffontaines, P. *Geographie et Religion* (Paris, 1948).

Donner, Fred. *The Early Islamic Conquests* (Princeton: Princeton University Press, 1981).

————. *Al-Takuin al-Tarikhi L-Lumah al-Arabiyah* (Beirut: Markaz Derasat al-Wehdah al-Arabiyah, 1984).

Duri, Abdel Aziz. "Government Institutions." In *The Islamic City*, R. B. Sergeant, ed. (Paris: UNESCO, 1980).

Eickelman, Dale. *The Middle East: An Anthropological Approach* (Englewood Cliffs, N.J.: Prentice-Hall, 1981).

El-Ali, Saleh. *Al-Tanzimat al-Ijtemauya wa al-Igtisadya Fi al-Basrah* (Beirut: Dar al-Talia'a, 1953).

————. "The Foundation of Baghdad." In *The Islamic City*, A. Hourani and S. M. Stern, eds. (Oxford: Bruno Cassirer, 1970).

Elisseeff, Nikita. "Dimashk." In *Encyclopedia of Islam* (Leiden: E. J. Brill, 1965), vol. 2.

Fischel, William. "The City in Islam." In *Middle Eastern Affairs* 7 (1956).

Gaube, Heinz. *Iranian Cities* (New York: New York University Press, 1979).

Gayer, P. *Itinera Hierosolymitana* Saeculi iv-viii.

Germen, A., ed. *Islamic Architecture and Urbanism* (Damman: King Faisal University, 1983).

Glubb, John. *A Short History of the Arab Peoples* (New York: Stein and Day, 1969).

Goitein, S. *Studies in Islamic History and Institutions* (Leiden: 1966).

Grabar, Oleg. "The Architecture of the Middle Eastern City." In *Middle Eastern Cities*, Ira Lapidus, ed. (Berkeley: University of California Press, 1969).

—————. *The Formation of Islamic Art* (New Haven: Yale University Press, 1973).

—————. "Three Seasons of Excavations at Qasr Al-Hayr Al-Sharqi." In *Ars Orientalis* 8 (1970).

————— and Richard Ettinghausen. *The Art and Architecture of Islam* (New York: Pelican History of Art — Pelican Books, 1987).

—————, Renata Holod, Jane Knustad, and William Trousdale. *City in the Desert* (Cambridge, Ma.: Harvard Middle Eastern Monographs, 1978).

Hakim, Besim. *Arabic-Islamic Cities* (London: Kegan Paul, 1986).

Hamdan, Gamal. "The Pattern of Medieval Urbanism in the Arab World." In *Geography*, 47 (1962).

Haswell, C. J. "Cairo: Origin and Development." In *Bulletin de la Societe Royal de Geographie d'Egypte*, 3 and 4 (1933).

Al-Hathloul, Saleh. *Tradition, Continuity and Change in the Physical Environment: The Arab Muslim City* (Ann Arbor: UMI, 1981).

Herzfeld, E. *Archaologische Reise im Euphrat und Tigris Gebiet* (Berlin: 1921).

Hinds, Martin, "Kufan Political Alignments and their Background in the Mid 7th Century." In *International Journal of Middle Eastern Studies*, vol. 2, no. 1 (1971).

Hitti, Philip. *Capital Cities of Arab Islam* (Minneapolis: University of Minnesota Press, 1973).

Hodgson, Marshall. *The Venture of Islam* (Chicago: University of Chicago Press, 1974), vol. 2.

Hourani, Albert, and S. M. Stern, eds. *The Islamic City* (Oxford: Bruno Cassirer, 1970).

—————. "The Islamic City in Light of Recent Research." In *The Islamic City*, Albert Hourani and S. M. Stern, eds. (Oxford: Bruno Cassirer, 1970).

Ismail, Adel. *Origin, Ideology and Physical Pattern of Arab Urbanization* (Karsruhe: University Dissertations, 1969).

Jairazbhoy, R. *Art and Cities of Islam* (New York: Asia Publishing House, 1965).

Al-Janabi, Kazem. *Takhtit Madinat al-Kufah* (Baghdad: Ministry of Culture, 1967).

Kanabar, Wadih. *Continuity of Spatial Change in Arabic Islamic Cities* (Ann Arbor: UMI, 1984).

Kuban, Dogan. "The Geographical and Historical Bases of the Diversity of Muslim Architectural Styles." In *Islamic Architecture and Urbanism*, A. German, ed.

(Dammam: King Faisal University Press, 1963).

Lapidus, Ira. "Evolution of Early Muslim Urban Society." In *Comparative Studies in Society and History*, Vol. 15, no. 1 (January 1973), pp. 21—50.

—————. *A History of Islamic Societies* (Cambridge: Cambridge University Press, 1988).

—————. "Muslim Settlement Policy during the Early Ummayad and Abbasid Caliphate." In *The Islamic Middle East*, A. Udovitch, ed. (Princeton: Darwin Press, 1981).

—————. "Muslim Cities and Islamic Societies." In *Middle Eastern Cities*, Ira Lapidus, ed. (Berkeley: University of California Press, 1969).

—————. *Muslim Cities in the Later Middle Ages* (Cambridge: Harvard University Press, 1967).

—————. "Traditional Muslim Cities: Structure and Change." In *From Madina to Metropolis*, L. Carl Brown, ed. (Princeton: Darwin Press, 1973).

Laroui, Abdullah. *The Crisis of the Arab Intellectual: Traditionalism or Historicism*, translated by D. Dammell (Berkeley: University of California Press, 1976).

—————. "Pour une methodologie des etudes islamiques: L'Islam au miroir de Gustave Von Grunebaum." In *Diogene 38* (July—September, 1973).

Lassner, Jacob. "The Caliph's Personal Domain." In *The Islamic City*, A. Hourani and S. M. Stern, eds. (Oxford: Bruno Cassirer, 1970).

—————. *The Shaping of Abbasid Rule* (Princeton: Princeton University Press, 1980).

—————. *The Topography of Baghdad in the Early Middle Ages* (Detroit: Wayne State University Press, 1970).

Leacroft, Helen, and Richard Leacroft. *The Buildings of Early Islam* (Reading, PA.: Addison-Wesley, 1979).

LeStrange, Guy. *Baghdad During the Abbasid Caliphate* (Oxford: Clarendon Press, 1900).

LeTourneau, Roger. *Fez in the Age of the Marinides* (Norman: University of Oklahoma Press, 1961).

—————. *Les Villes Musulmanes des L'Afrique du Nord* (Algiers, 1957).

Lev, Yaacov. "Army, Regime and Society in Fatimid Egypt." In *International Journal of Middle Eastern Studies 19*, no. 3 (August, 1987).

Levy, Reuben. *A Baghdad Chronicle* (Cambridge: Cambridge University Press, 1929).

Llewelyn, Othman. "Shariah Values Pertaining to Landscape Planning and Design." In *Islamic Architecture and Urbanism*, A. Germen, ed. (Dammam: King Faisal University Press, 1983).

Lynch, Kevin, and Lloyd Rodwin. "The Form of the City." In *Cities and City Planning*, Lloyd Rodwin, ed. (New York: Plenum Press, 1981).

Massignon, Louis, "Explication du plan de Kufa." In *Melange Maspero* (Paris: 1937).

—————. "Sinf." In *Encyclopedia of Islam* (London: 1956), vol. 4.

Marcais, George. "La Conception des villes dans L'Islam." *Revue d'Alger* (Algiers, 1945).

—————. "L'Urbanisme Musulmane." In *Congres de la Federation des Societes Savantes de L'Afrique du Nord* (Algiers, 1940).

Marcais, William. "L'Islamisme et la Vie Urbaine." In *L'Academie des inscriptions et belles-lettres: Comptes Rendus* (Paris) 1928.

Monier, Ahmed. *Cities of Islam* (Beirut: B.A.U. Press, 1971).

Morony, Michael. *Iraq After the Muslim Conquest* (Princeton: Princeton University Press, 1984).

Al-Munjid, Salah. *Tarik Mandinat Demashq* (Damascus: Dar al-Ketab, 1961).

Al-Musawi, Mustafa. *Al-'Awamel al-Tarikhiyah L-nasha'at wa Tatur al-Mudun al-Arabiyah al-Islamiyah* (Baghdad: Ministry of Culture, 1982).

Mustafa, Saleh L. *Al-Madinah al-Munawarah* (Beirut: Dar al-Nahdah al-Arabiyah, 1981).

Noe, Samuel. "In Search of 'The' Traditional Islamic City: An Analytical Proposal with Lahore as a Case Example." In *Ekistics, 280*, (Jan.—Feb. 1980).

Pauty, E. "Villes spontanees et villes crees en Islam." In *Annales de L'Institute d'Etude Orientals 9* (1950).

Popenoe, David. "On the Meaning of Urban." In *Urbanism, Urbanization, and Change: Comparative Perspectives*, P. Meadows and E. Mizurchi, eds. (Reading, Pa.: Addison-Wesley, 1976).

Reitemeyer, R. *Beschreibung Agyptens* (Leipzig, 1903).

Renan, Ernest. "Histoire Generale et Systeme de Langues semitique." In *Oeuvres Completes* (Paris, 1840).

Al-Rihawi, Abdul-Kader. *Madinat Demashq* (Damascus: Al-Majaz, 1969).

Sabanum, Ahmad. *Demashq Fi Dawa'er al-Ma'aref* (Damascus: Dar al-Keta al-Arabi, 1986).

Said, Edward. *Orientalism* (New York: Vintage Books, 1979).

Salem, El Sayed A. *Al-Tarikh al-Siyasi wa al-Hadari LL-Dawlah al-Arabiyah* (Beirut: Dar al-Nahdah, 1987).

Salibi, Kamal. *Syria Under Islam* (New York: Caravan Books, 1977).

Saggaf, Abdul Aziz, ed. *The Middle East City* (New York: Paragon House, 1987).

Sauvaget, Jean. "Le Plan Antique de Damas." In *Syria 26* (1949).

————. *Alep* (Paris: Librairie Orientaliste, 1941).

————. "Le Plan de Laodicee-Sur-Mer." In *Bulletin d'Etude Orientals* (Paris: 1934), vol. 4.

————. "Esquisse d'une histoire de la ville de Damas." In *Revue Etudes Islamiques 3* (1934).

Serageldin, Ismail and Samer El-Sadek, eds. *The Arab City* (Riyadh: Arab Urban Development Institute, 1982).

Serjeant, R. B., ed. *The Islamic City* (London: UNESCO, 1980).

Shaeban, M. *Islamic History: A New Interpretation* (Cambridge: Cambridge University Press, 1976).

Shalabi, Ahmad. *Musu'at al-Tarikh wa al-Hadarah al-Islamiyah* (Cairo: Maktabat al-Anglo al-Misriyah, 1974).

Smith, C. T. *An Historical Geography of Western Europe* (London: Longman, 1967).

Stern, S. M. "The Constitution of the Islamic City." In *The Islamic City*, A. Hourani and S. Stern, eds. (Oxford: Bruno Cassirer, 1970).

Taha, A. D. *Al-Fateh Wa al-Isteqrar al-Arabi al-Islami fi Shamal Ifrigiyah wa al-Andalus* (Baghdad: Ministry of Culture: 1982).

Trancik, Roger. *Finding Lost Space* (New York: Van Nostrand Reinhold, 1986).

Von Grunebaum, Gustave. *Islam: Essays in the Nature and Growth of a Cultural Tradition* (London: Routledge and Kegan Paul, 1955).

Wagstaff, J. M. "The Origin and Evolution of Towns." In *The Changing Middle Eastern City*, G. H. Balke and R. J. Lawless, eds. (London: Crown Helm, 1983).

Weber, Max. *The City*. translated by D. Martindale and G. Newirth (Glenco, 1958).

Wheatly, Paul. "The Concept of Urbanism." In *Man, Settlement and Urbanism*, Peter Ucko and Roger Tringham, eds. (London: Longman, 1967).

Zaki, Abdul Rahman. *Al-Qahirah 969—1825* (Cairo: Al-Dar al-Mesriyah L'Lta'lif wa al-Targamah, 1966).

Zaydan, Jurji. *Tarikh al-Tamadun al-Islami* (Cairo: Al-Helal Press, 1904).

INDEX

ABOUT THE AUTHOR

NEZAR ALSAYYAD is an architect, planner and urban historian. He is currently Assistant Professor of Architecture at the University of California, Berkeley, where he teaches courses on third world housing, urban design and history of Islamic Architecture. His other books include *The Streets of Islamic Cairo* and *Dwellings, Settlements and Tradition.*

RECENT TITLES IN
CONTRIBUTIONS TO THE STUDY OF WORLD HISTORY

Young Guard! The Communist Youth League, Petrograd 1917–1920
Isabel A. Tirado

Tsar Paul and the Question of Madness: An Essay in History and Psychology
Hugh Ragsdale

Ritual and Record: Sports Records and Quantification in Pre-Modern Societies
John Marshall Carter and Arnd Krüger, editors

Diverse Paths to Modernity in Southeastern Europe: Essays in National Development
Gerasimos Augustinos, editor